Thirty-Seven Myths about Marriage

Thirty-Seven Myths about Marriage

What I Think I Know and What I Wish I Knew

ALAN J. HOVESTADT *and*
KENNETH W. SCHMIDT

Forewords by Brian S. Canfield and
Karen B. Helmeke and *Gary H. Bischof*

RESOURCE *Publications* · Eugene, Oregon

THIRTY-SEVEN MYTHS ABOUT MARRIAGE
What I Think I Know and What I Wish I Knew

Resource Publications
An Imprint of Wipf and Stock Publishers
199 W. 8th Ave., Suite 3
Eugene, OR 97401

www.wipfandstock.com

PAPERBACK ISBN: 978-1-6667-4890-1
HARDCOVER ISBN: 978-1-6667-4891-8
EBOOK ISBN: 978-1-6667-4892-5

08/19/22

Contents

Foreword

Thirty-Seven Myths about Marriage uses a light and humorous touch to offer a wealth of knowledge and insight for individuals and couples who wish to gain a greater understanding of marriage and the typical challenges that couples face. Drawing upon decades of teaching and clinical experience in helping hundreds of couples, Alan Hovestadt and Kenneth Schmidt offer a wealth of knowledge, practical suggestions, and guidance for individuals thinking about marriage, for couples who have a stable marriage and wish to increase their understanding and happiness, and for couples struggling with marital issues.

Thirty-Seven Myths about Marriage offers valuable insights to anyone, professional and layperson alike, who wants to better understand the irrational beliefs, common fallacies, and assumptions about marriage that often lead to misunderstandings, growing dissatisfaction, and problems that couples can't seem to resolve.

A common "myth," particularly in many western societies, is that each of us is destined to find that one special person who will fulfill us and make us happy despite the inevitable trials of life. When this myth becomes apparent, one or both partners may become disillusioned—often questioning their choice of a mate and even the continuation of their relationship. However, despite this common occurrence, the institution of marriage remains extremely popular. The overwhelming majority of people will marry at least once in their lifetime. Of those who divorce, statistically the majority will remarry a second and even a third time. The desire to find the "right one" is persistent, but often the ingrained myths about marriage endure, leading to a repeat of the same problems in subsequent relationships.

Historically, couples remain together for a multitude of reasons. These include economic and lifestyle considerations, religious commitment, an effort to maintain an intact family unit for children, and other practical or social considerations. While there are numerous reasons that people leave their marriage, it's common to see increased dissatisfaction along with a social acceptance and ease to get a divorce. Second and third marriages experience an even higher rate of divorce. In the year 1900, approximately one in nineteen marriages ended in divorce in the USA. By the 1950s, the rate of marital dissolution had increased to approximately one out five, and by the 1980s the rate of divorce had increased to just under 50 percent of all marriages.

It is crucial for individuals and couples to realize that the beliefs they hold influence why they marry, and what they expect in their marriage. This is critical for helping them address and effectively resolve their marital concerns. The challenge is not so much to find a way to prevent divorce, but to help couples find effective ways to increase sustainable marital satisfaction.

Thirty-Seven Myths about Marriage helps couples uncover those beliefs. They can begin to see how their beliefs are detrimental to their relationship and adjust them accordingly. I am glad to see the publication of this book, and honored to make this small contribution to promote its success.

Brian S. Canfield, Ed.D.
Professor of Clinical Mental Health Counseling
Florida Atlantic University
Past President, International Association
of Marriage and Family Counseling
Fellow and Past President, American Counseling Association

Mythbusters

When a young engaged couple has unrealistic expectations about marriage, or partners are constrained by idealistic societal assumptions about committed relationships, "Who you gonna call? . . . Mythbusters!" Much like the Ghostbusters in the classic comedy movie, Alan Hovestadt and Kenneth Schmidt use wit and humor to challenge many commonly held beliefs about marriage and committed relationships. This collection of myths is written in a fun and lighthearted manner that is accessible and easy to read, yet readers will walk away not only thinking about their views on relationships, but they will also acquire some practical pointers for how to enhance their relationships. *Thirty-Seven Myths* is ideal for couples who are in the beginning of their committed lives together or who are contemplating being in a serious relationship with someone. The book may also help those who have been married or together for some time.

This book challenges thirty-seven common myths about relationships, and the authors discuss each one in a spritely and informative way. Each chapter is about three pages long, and follows a consistent format. The first section is called "Mythical Thinking," and we suggest three cautions for readers. First, watch out for the sarcasm in this section of each chapter! The authors use a playful, humorous, tongue-in-cheek tone in this section, not meant to be taken literally. A second caution: you may find yourself having a hearty laugh or two as you recognize yourself, your partner, or someone else you know when reading through this section. A third caution is that reading this section may expose and challenge the reader's assumptions about relationships. If you do not want your thinking challenged, skip this part, skip the book, don't bother getting married, etc.!

The second section of each chapter/myth is titled "On Second Thought . . ." and in this section the authors offer antidotes, avuncular advice, and research-based commentary to counter and challenge our mythical thinking about relationships.

The third section of each chapter/myth is titled "Parting Thought," and contains a thought-provoking, amusing, or inspiring quotation that highlights the authors' thoughts regarding the myth. Those quoted include columnist Ann Landers, comedian Phyllis Diller, poet Khalil Gibran, and relationship therapist and expert Brené Brown.

The fourth section of each chapter/myth is titled "Further Reflections" which offers questions for pondering or discussing. The best part of these questions is that none of them have any definite, absolute answers, but are a means for identifying areas of difference and agreement.

The thirty-seven myths are presented in four sections of the book: six of the myths are in "Your Dream Marriage"; eight of the myths are in "Seeking Your Perfect Partner for Your Perfect Marriage"; the bulk of the thirty-seven myths are in the third section of the book, called "Living Your Dream Marriage"; and there are four myths in "Your Dream Marriage: Paradise Lost."

The first part, "Your Dream Marriage," is a helpful part of the book to read even before you are in a serious relationship, and will help you better understand what some of your ideas and expectations are of what a good relationship and marriage should be. The second part of the book, "Seeking Your Perfect Partner for Your Perfect Marriage," will give you some humorous glimpses into the challenges that can occur when you first meet "the one" or someone you would like to share your life with. The third part of the book, "Living Your Dream Marriage," focuses on ways that a couple can build a long-lasting foundation for their life together and discusses some of the distorted thinking that gets in the way. In the four myths in the fourth part of the book, "Your Dream Marriage: Paradise Lost," the authors address the inevitable ups and downs that occur in any long-term relationship and provide some encouragement to counter the hurt and disillusionment that can come during these periods.

We suggest some ways readers can use this book. Each partner might ponder the questions in the "For Further Reflection" section at the end of each chapter/myth after reading the chapter and prior to discussing them with each other. A couple could also read through the book together and use it as a discussion starter. For couples newly engaged or married, they could select one chapter/myth a week and set aside time to read and discuss the chapter with each other.

Partners could also quiz their friends or family to see how they would answer these questions and how they handled the kinds of situations discussed in each chapter. Readers could also use *Thirty-Seven Myths* in conjunction with premarital counseling. A premarital counselor could give a list of the thirty-seven myths to each partner at the beginning of their work together and have them check off the ones they agree with. A couple could raise with their premarital counseling facilitator any areas where a difference of opinion between the two of them emerged. *Thirty-Seven Myths* would also be useful for marriage and couple therapists who are working with couples, providing another framework for therapists to identify and name some of the ways couples may get stuck. Finally, this book can also make a great wedding gift!

As married partners who both hold a Ph.D. in Marriage and Family Therapy, and who have taught Couple Therapy courses for decades, and counseled numerous couples with a wide range of presenting issues, we find this book refreshing and useful to challenge many commonly held myths about marriage and committed relationships. It is easy to imagine the authors, with their extensive experience, talking with couples about these myths in couple therapy or premarital counseling, with a wry smile or twinkle in their eyes! *Thirty-Seven Myths* offers the wonderful opportunity for couples to learn from the decades of experience of these master "Mythbusters!"

Karen B. Helmeke, Ph.D., LMFT
Private Practice Couple and Family Therapist and
Adjunct Professor, Western Michigan University

Gary H. Bischof, Ph.D., LMFT
Professor, Department of Counselor Education and Counseling
Psychology, Western Michigan University, and Coordinator of the
Master's Program in Marriage, Couple, and Family Counseling

Introduction

What is marriage? What is marriage really like? Statistics suggest that "happily ever after" occurs no more than 50 percent of the time, considering how many couples divorce. Is it like the movies, and if so, *which* movies?—there are so many possibilities! How many marriages are like your parents' marriage? Is that a good thing?

What do *you* think marriage is really like? And why do you think that? Because of what you read? or dreamed about? or hoped for? Because of your experience with dating, or living together, or being married, or even being married more than once? Because of the experience you've seen or heard about from couples?

Marriage is a pretty common experience. It's all around us; it's existed through most of human history and in almost all cultures. Most people get married at some point in their life. Why do they *do* that? What are they looking for? What do they hope to get? Why not just live together? Or date forever?

This book is not about answering those questions. It does assume that, if push came to shove, you have your own answers to those questions. Not answers supplied by religious leaders, or researchers, or therapists, but answers from your gut, based on what you have seen and heard and think you know based on your experience.

Those ideas and beliefs are in your head right now. You may be aware of them, or they may be buried—but they're there. It doesn't matter whether you're single, playing the field, celibate, hooking up, commitment-phobic, in a serious relationship, recovering from a breakup, living together, married, divorced, or widowed. The thoughts and assumptions and opinions and values that you have about marriage are guiding your actions and influencing your relationships every day.

There are lots of words that can be used to characterize those thoughts, such as ideas, dreams, judgments, presumptions, evaluations, or conclusions. If someone had the time and inclination, they could interview you or give you a survey and figure out which of your thoughts are more or less similar to thoughts of others. Some of them may be "spot on" and others may be "off the wall."

Experience suggests that a fair number of people have expectations and beliefs about marriage that aren't very realistic. There are lots of ways to say that—messy thinking, distorted cognition, stinkin' thinkin', denial, ignorance, and false conclusions, to name a few. And if you start off with unrealistic expectations, you are likely to end up very disappointed, whether you're starting to date or in a long-term relationship.

You may then experience incongruity between your lived experience and what you expect (or hope for, want, or need); the expectations don't match up with your reality. In addition, American society has radically increased its general expectations of marriage, so that many people are looking for the one person who can fulfill their every want and need and provide them with a very high level of life-satisfaction until they die.

We subscribe to many of the beliefs articulated by some of the 20th century's preeminent psychotherapists, including Albert Ellis, Aaron Beck, and Donald Meichenbaum. For example, Ellis noted that *irrational beliefs* lead to unrealistic expectations, which then result in annoyance, discomfort, and upheaval. Ellis suggested that the resolution to our emotional distress comes when we look carefully at what we're saying to ourselves. The "cure," according to these practitioners, is to help clients correct their distorted thinking, develop *more rational beliefs*, and change their behavior accordingly.

This book has collected a large number of "irrational" beliefs and ideas. We call them "myths" because they are widely held but false or flawed ideas. Like some myths, they contain some truth (or we would have dumped them). Therefore, myths continue to guide personal and social behavior. If you believe a "myth" about marriage, it influences how you select the people you date, and how you interact with prospective partners and your spouse(s).

One cautionary note—at some point you may experience a serious temptation to proclaim (in your head or even out loud) that "X is not a myth!" You may have heard someone sincerely state that myth; or perhaps you read it on the internet somewhere; or maybe you know a couple like that and it doesn't seem to be a problem. It's just possible that you believe that myth yourself, and that can be a shock. Just because you can't see it's a problem doesn't mean it isn't. Try reading the *Mythical Thinking* and then see what you think.

It's a temptation to disregard a myth because it strikes close to home. Sometimes we may be tempted to disregard a myth that really scares us, and that may be the most dangerous act of all.

We hope you enjoy the book, and even chuckle a few times. We hope that you gain a few insights, and learn a thing or two about yourself and your relationship. Perhaps you'll recognize yourself somewhere along the way, and it will provoke a heart-to-heart conversation with your partner about a difficult topic. You may decide to get some assistance; you don't have to wait until things become *big problems*. Go ahead and try out some new ways to behave, so that your marriage can be more like you would like it to be.

Your Dream Marriage

Thinking about marriage occurs long before the wedding, and even before a serious relationship.

Your brain is recording memories of parents, grandparents, aunts and uncles and cousins, the parents and grandparents of your friends, as well as your neighbors, and people you see in stores. (Probably not your teachers, though, because in your young mind they have no life outside the school.)

You are also flooded with a variety of images from television and movies. You hear hundreds of jokes from comedians about what marriage is like. You watch a Hallmark movie and know how it will turn out in the first five minutes, and you hear news reports tell you about spousal abuse.

From all of that, your mind picks and chooses images of what you think marriage will be like, what your future spouse will be like. And then you try to make that dream come true.

PARTING THOUGHT

"When two people are under the influence of the most violent, most insane, most delusive, and most transient of passions, they are required to swear that they will remain in that excited, abnormal, and exhausting condition continuously until death do them part."[1]

---

1. Shaw, "Preface."

1

Marriage Should Be Totally Happy All the Time

MYTHICAL THINKING

Isn't one of the reasons for getting married to secure your happiness? If you're happy at least some of the time when you're *not* married, then it seems marriage should boost the happiness factor to the top of the chart; otherwise, why bother getting married?

In order to preserve this happiness, you must always have a smile on your face. More importantly, you must be sure to hide anything that is uncomfortable or unpleasant because it threatens your unending happiness. You must deny that there is anything about the other person that irritates you or that you disagree with, because that also threatens your perpetual happiness. You live in a state of high alert, watching for any threat to your relationship that can lead to a disastrous outcome.

At some point one of those thoughts leaks out, or perhaps you have a fight. Omigosh! Your relationship suddenly is doomed to fail because at this very moment the happiness has vanished. There's great fear that the wonderful times you've enjoyed were somehow fraudulent memories, the plans or fantasies about your future were simply a house of cards built on quicksand, and everything around you is crumbling. Perhaps at that moment, you realize that nothing is real, you have been duped, and it's best to walk away before you suffer any more. Run! Hide! Best to save yourself more heartache and get out before it's too late.

ON SECOND THOUGHT . . .

Have you ever met a couple who were totally happy all the time? If this myth were true, it seems like you would have met at least a few such couples at some point in your life. But if you scratch the surface, you'll see every one of us is a flesh and blood human being who is not perfect, and none of us is happy all the time, whether we're married or not.

Getting out of a relationship at the first sign of trouble is one option. Sticking around and having a discussion about your differences is another option.

There may be some underlying assumptions with this myth:

If you really love each other, then you'll always be happy.

If you're best friends, then you'll always be happy.

If you do it right (whatever *that* means), then you'll always be happy.

Your own life experience, no matter how long you have lived, should help you to accept that none of these assumptions are true.

One of the issues in this myth is that it is loaded with extreme thinking—*totally* happy, *all the time,* and *disaster.* Those are really high expectations and awful consequences. Finding happiness is an understandable goal; being happy every moment of every day is neither realistic nor attainable despite your best efforts.

So what if your expectation is—Marriage can be reasonably happy a fair amount of the time, and sometimes marriage includes things that are uncomfortable or difficult, which usually can be managed, and occasionally requires some assistance.

PARTING THOUGHT

"All marriages are happy; it's living together afterward that's tough."[1]

FOR FURTHER REFLECTION

Are there things that you fake or hide from your partner? What reasons do you say to yourself for doing that?

What percentage of time do you and your partner think that you'll be happy? If you disagree, what are you going to do next?

If it's your goal, what could each of you do that would increase your happiness?

---

1. Landers, *The Ann Landers Encyclopedia*, 712.

2

There's Never Disagreement
in a Happy Marriage

MYTHICAL THINKING

This is a measuring stick you must use to evaluate a future partner. As soon as you find out that you disagree about something, you will know that your relationship is not going to work.

People have different size rulers, though. Some people discard a potential partner when there's any disagreement at all—"I like bubble gum and my partner likes Juicy Fruit." Others permit a little wiggle room—"I prefer tacos while my partner prefers tostadas, and we can live with that." Some tolerate even bigger disagreements, allowing Coke and Pepsi cans to occupy the same refrigerator. But as soon as they disagree on anything that one of them deems "serious," they conclude that it's time to get out. There's no need to talk about it, because it's clear they disagree, and therefore they can't stay together. The mere existence of a disagreement is like a colony of termites that will eat away at the foundation of their relationship until it crumbles.

If you manage to get through the whole courtship, engagement, and wedding without any disagreement, Congratulations! You're on your way to being a perfect couple who will live happily ever after.

But . . . what if a disagreement emerges *after* the wedding? Was everything before that a big fat lie? Was someone hiding something, or worse, lying about it?

You must hide this, immediately! Do not let anyone know that you disagree with one another. They will laugh at you, despise you, and cut you out of their will. You will be a disgrace to your extended family, and your friends will abandon you rather than take the chance that they could catch the disagreement-virus themselves.

In order to survive this catastrophic development, this caterpillar-myth must transform itself into a butterfly-myth—*Never let anyone find out that you disagree.* All your disagreements must take place behind closed doors (it's better when off the property; and best in a secluded place like northern Canada). Your children must never find out that you disagreed. Otherwise, you will have failed them by not providing the perfect example they deserve and expect of their parents.

ON SECOND THOUGHT . . .

There's a chance that you won't have any disagreements, statistically about 1 in 78,000,000,000,000,000,000,000,000,000 (seventy-eight billion trillion). No two people are aligned so well that they're not going to run into ideas, decisions, even values where they're not in unison. It's to be expected.

Here's another statistic: 69 percent of issues are not totally resolved! So here's another myth: *Arguing is normal and healthy.* Unfortunately that statement is not true standing on its own. Research tells us that whether disagreeing is normal and healthy depends on *how* you argue and *what* you argue about. Because more than two-thirds of issues don't get resolved, it becomes clear that there are other factors to be considered beyond whether people disagree.

Disagreements can flow from misunderstandings because *opinions are not facts*; they often get confused. A disagreement about whether Venus or Mars is closer to the earth can be resolved by a quick visit to Wikipedia to get the facts. A disagreement about how to spend a Friday evening involves opinions about what people think they will enjoy.

The disagreements can also vary in their level of importance and consequence. You may disagree how to clean a stain in the carpet, and you can disagree about how to discipline children. One can result in a permanent stain, while the other can result in healthy or traumatized children.

How you look at your differences makes all the difference. a) Are your differences so far apart that they cannot coexist? For example, one of you wants a large family and the other one doesn't want any kids. For some spouses, disagreements could revolve around significant religious differences. b) Are your differences things that can exist side by side? There are couples who disagree about the use of alcohol, but they learn to live with each other's drinking or abstinence. Or sticking with the theme of drinking, one partner finds it disgusting that the other one drinks right out of the milk container, so they resolve it by having his and her containers. c) Are your differences two ideas that can be combined into something new? "I wanted a ranch and my spouse wanted a two-story home with a basement and attic. So the architect designed a home where we can live comfortably on the main floor, and we created other spaces in the second-story and the basement for an office, hobbies, guests, and storage."

The disagreements in themselves may not be the issue as much as how you perceive them. Think about music—harmony requires at least two different notes, as opposed to unison when all the singers and instruments are on the same note. There can be harmonies that are beautiful with full rich sounds created with many different notes; there can also be discordant harmony when two notes don't go well together (at least according to one person's ear). We also know that we can enjoy harmonies now that past generations found discordant; we can get used to different sounds.

So disagreements that are considered to be abominations which must be obliterated will probably be destructive to a relationship if they are not resolved. Disagreements thought of as different notes that can create harmonic music have the potential to enrich a relationship as the partners listen, learn, and adapt to one another.

Couples can learn to make beautiful music together.

PARTING THOUGHT

"Marriage should be a duet—when one sings, the other claps."[1]

FOR FURTHER REFLECTION

What feelings do disagreements provoke in you? How much disagreement (emotionally and intellectually) can you tolerate?

Is there room in your relationship for disagreement? Do you hide disagreements to keep the peace? What price might you pay for that later, i.e., what could the consequences be if your spouse finds out that you actually disagree about that particular topic?

Are there topics or issues that absolutely rule out a relationship for you, e.g., I could never be with a person who thinks (or does) _____."

---

1. Murray, *AZ Quotes.*

3

Total Honesty Leads to Marital Paradise

MYTHICAL THINKING

How could anyone be opposed to honesty? It's a virtue!

It's also the foundation for any healthy relationship. Honesty is what allows people to trust one another rather than wondering if they have been misled. Being trustworthy and believing your partner is trustworthy are both essential components for building a secure and long-lasting marriage.

Only someone with something to hide would refuse to be totally honest. Which just proves the point that total honesty is to be expected and necessary. So necessary that its presence in the marriage will guarantee your marital utopia because it is built on the bedrock of trust and total honesty.

ON SECOND THOUGHT . . .

Total honesty may seem like an honorable behavior, but is it?

When someone asks, "Do these jeans make me look fat?" does the question require a totally honest answer? The wise husband had been married for many years when his wife came to him so happy and said, "Look, dear! I bought this the first year we were married and it still fits!" He kept his mouth shut. (It was a scarf.)

Sometimes a question is a trap that you can't even answer without getting twisted in a knot: "Do you still beat your spouse?" Even a "no" answer suggests that you used to beat your spouse, but don't do it anymore.

And sometimes a question doesn't even require a response at all, much less total honesty. If a stranger asks you, "How's your sex life?" it's none of their business, and you don't owe them a totally honest response. (Just because someone asks you a question doesn't mean you have to give them an answer.)

There is a difference between dishonesty and simply sparing someone pain. Deliberately dishonest behaviors (including lying, deliberately misleading, deceiving, and withholding information) at a minimum are unethical and immoral, and at times they may even be criminal.

On the other hand, lying, misleading, deception, and withholding may be selfish behaviors in order to keep control, maintain the upper hand, or achieve a personal goal at the expense of the other person. Someone may be deliberately hurtful under the guise of being honest.

Sometimes "being truthful" is really just sharing an opinion. "That is an ugly shirt" or "Your haircut makes you look like a nerd" are matters of opinion, not facts.

Answering a question honestly can be done in more than one way. "Do these jeans make me look fat?" "They sure do!" may be honest; it's also hurtful. And hurtful can be damaging. An honest response might be, "I think you have some pants that are more flattering to your figure." Or even, "If that's a question in your own mind, you might want to wear something else today."

As a general principle, the virtue of honesty is valuable and a preferred option. And there may be times when it's better just to keep your mouth shut!

PARTING THOUGHT

"People who are brutally honest get more satisfaction out of the brutality than out of the honesty."[1]

FOR FURTHER REFLECTION

Have you ever had experiences where you were honest and it blew up in your face? What conclusions do you draw from that?

Are there times when you should (or should not) be honest when you suspect it is going to hurt your partner or damage your relationship?

Are there occasions when lying is OK to your partner? Is there a difference between lying, not saying anything, and misleading? Are there appropriate times for any of those behaviors? What are the possible outcomes?

---

1. Needham, *AZ Quotes*.

4

Successful Marital Partners Should Be like Twins Who Have Everything in Common

MYTHICAL THINKING

Couples might not start out as mirror images of one another, yet surely that's the goal. As your marital union grows deeper roots, you should gradually begin to look alike, sound alike, and dress alike. You must laugh at the same jokes and tell the same stories from your vacation. All of your memories will coincide with no discrepancies between them. You will be amazed that even your dreams overlap. You will continue to act and feel just like you did when you started dating—always excited to be together, finding it difficult to be apart (different rooms in the same house is a strain), and unable to keep your hands off each other.

The result of this is you can totally rely on this one person because they are just like you. If you can't count on that, then they are of no use to you. The first time that they disagree or do something differently than you, dump the loser.

You've heard the expression that in marriage "the two have become one." Therefore it's dangerous to keep acting as if you are still two. Total similarity is the key; you must strive to be one in everything you think and say and do.

The attainment of this goal is so important that, if you don't achieve this status, your marriage is a complete failure.

ON SECOND THOUGHT . . .

First of all, a heads up—doing everything together actually requires the spouses to do a lot more negotiation and compromise. Even when they perform activities together, it's likely that the partners will also encounter personal differences within those activities. Let's say that both of them enjoy shopping together for groceries. However, one clips coupons and one thinks it's a waste of time; one buys impulsively and the other prepares a shopping list and sticks to it. They are going to have to figure out how they will grocery shop together.

There's really a bundle of beliefs related to this myth:

Partners should be like twins. ("like attracts like")

Partners should be very different. ("opposites attract")

Couples should do everything together.

Partners should always have their own interests.

Having common interests keeps spouses together.

Doing everything together drives spouses apart.

What the statements have in common is their all-or-nothing nature.

The fact is, having things in common or doing things together is fine. So is having your own interests and doing things on your own. Doing things together or doing things separately is not what strengthens a relationship or damages a relationship—it's *what* you are doing and *how* you interact that affects the relationship. For example:

- You may play board games together, and if one of you is a cut-throat, do-anything-to-win player, it's the harmful attitude directed at your partner that can hurt your relationship even though you're sharing an activity.

- One of you can enjoy riding a bike and the other playing video games. If one of you consistently chooses the hobby rather than spending some time with your spouse, it's the amount of time that you devote to the activity that's the issue, not that you're doing something different than your partner.

- You can share the same activity, like robbing banks. It's also not very good for your marriage when you're both incarcerated for ten years in different prisons.

- You can even do the same thing separately, which may seem like the best option of all. Maybe having his and her gardens is a good idea; both of you having extramarital affairs is not.

At the end of the day, it's OK to be your own person, and more interesting than being a mirror reflection of your spouse.

PARTING THOUGHT

"The only thing my husband and I have in common is that we were married on the same day."[1]

FOR FURTHER REFLECTIONS

What activities do you enjoy doing by yourself? And what activities do you enjoy doing with others?

What are your beliefs about spouses doing things together and separately?

Is doing things together the same thing as depending on one another? If not, how would you explain the difference?

1. Diller, *AZ Quotes.*

5

Doing Everything Together
Will Lead To Total Happiness

MYTHICAL THINKING

Any couple that's got something going loves spending time with one another. You find it painful to be separated even for a short period of time, and you excitedly anticipate the next time you will see each other. After all, what's the point of being a couple if you don't do everything *as a couple?* Family and friends know this too, and start to refer to you as a unit—TerryandMary, StacyandTracy. Real couples are practically joined at the hip, so you might as well be called Siamese twins.

It's not only that you *want* to do everything as a twosome. It's that you *know*, in your heart of hearts, that the key to your ultimate happiness is that you *like* being together. You enjoy every moment you spend together, and the more time, the better. Sadly, you are also absolutely miserable when you are apart, and will do almost anything to relieve your distress. You can't get enough of each other, and you look for more ways to adjust your schedule so that you can have more time to spend with each other. All of this is proof that you are meant for each other.

ON SECOND THOUGHT . . .

You are two people who truly enjoy one another's company. There is pleasure and excitement as you get to know someone more intimately, and as that other person gets to know you. Even better, they still like you and find you fascinating, and you are delighted as you explore the hidden mysteries of the other person. It's like the anticipation and joy of unwrapping a beautiful present.

Nevertheless, you are still two people; you most definitely are not Siamese twins. As you submerge yourselves into someone else's life, you also have to take time to come up for air. Getting to know your partner is not something that you will accomplish in weeks or months. Your spouse will be a parcel that surprises you and a mystery that sometimes confounds you even fifty years from now.

The intensity of all that togetherness can drain your emotional energy. "Hot and heavy" can turn into "lukewarm and commonplace." You may lose focus on some important things and even ignore your friends when you concentrate too much on the new person in your life.

The period of exploration can be difficult for some people. You might be comfortable having your own space, following your own schedule, and doing things your own way. Perhaps you take for granted how you usually do things, and then your new friend handles the situation differently.

In fact, you need to make adjustments to accommodate this new person in your life. Suddenly there's someone else to take into consideration. You are in their space and they are in yours. You have to consult before making plans. That may come as a wonderful surprise. But it could also be uncomfortable or upsetting.

Doing everything together may be a strain, and can feel like a loss of personal freedom. One or both of you may feel restricted or tied to an anchor. That in turn can lead to thinking, "Maybe this isn't as great as I thought," or "This is harder than I expected," especially if it's your first serious relationship. You might even feel disloyal to the other person because you had a thought about wanting some space for yourself.

Be at peace! It is normal and healthy to enjoy intimacy *and* to have time and space for yourself. In general, a good relationship is entered by gradual steps and not "all at once." Take your time and enjoy the process of getting to know another wonderful human being.

PARTING THOUGHT

"Let there be spaces in your togetherness, and let the winds of heaven blow between you . . . And stand together, yet not too near together: For the pillars of the temple stand apart, and the oak tree and the cypress grow not in each other's shadow."[1]

FOR FURTHER REFLECTION

How do you feel when the two of you are apart? How do you interpret that feeling or explain it to yourself?

When do you expect that you will really know and understand your partner completely? What will you have accomplished when that finally happens?

Do you sometimes feel as you are too deeply submerged in your life *together*, and you have disappeared? If that happens, what would you like to do?

1. Gibran, "On Marriage," 15.

6

When Spouses Sacrifice All Their Own Needs, Their Marriage Will Thrive

MYTHICAL THINKING

Your willingness to sacrifice yourself is noble. Your eagerness to give up having your needs satisfied is absolutely heroic. Your readiness to set aside all your personal desires is altruistic to the nth degree. It's amazing that you weren't married by the time you were sixteen, because whoever gets you gets a saint.

Fortunately for you and your spouse, you realized early on that this is what marriage requires of you—totally giving yourself to your partner. Nothing must be held back. You must pay for everything that will make your partner happy—their education, their big toys, and their shopping expeditions. Paying for your spouse to go on vacations with friends makes sense because you know those friendships are so important to your partner; really, it's fine that you stay behind to take care of all the things that need taking caring of. In the end, even bankruptcy is not too big a price to pay if you can make your partner happy.

You also realized that when you get married, your time is no longer your own. All your time must be devoted to your spouse. You can run all the errands because your spouse is occupied with work and hobbies and the gym and his social life. It's wonderful that your spouse is so dedicated to a balanced lifestyle, and that you can dedicate all of your time to taking care of everything else in your lives, including your home and your children and the finances and the shopping and the laundry and the yardwork. You know in your heart of hearts that you're not a *slave* so much as a loyal and trusted *servant* of your beloved.

Keeping your partner happy is a worthy goal. Yet you know that there's a higher purpose to which only a select few spouses are called. Some of you have been given the awesome responsibility of saving your spouse. That special person needs *you*, and will not survive if you don't do everything necessary to secure their rescue. Your perseverance in this life-long task even more praiseworthy and vital, because we're talking about *saving a life*.

And it doesn't hurt that your heroic behavior guarantees a lifelong marriage, because your partner is obligated to stay with you because of all the sacrifices you've made.

ON SECOND THOUGHT . . .

Seriously, some people have suffered greatly as children. Some prospective spouses have disabilities, life challenges, and diseases that limit their abilities. Some of you may be ready to choose a partner and accept those challenges and constraints.

However, remember you have neither the responsibility nor the strength to save anyone. No one has that much power. It's a horrible thing to do that to yourself—to take on that task and assume that's what marriage demands of you. In some religious circles you may hear, "We already have a savior, and it's not you."

Marriage is a partnership, in which the spouses are dedicated to one another. There should be a give and take within a context of equality. It won't necessarily be fifty-fifty, and may even vary over time, but in general a healthy relationship will have a balance of power.

Marriage is not a relationship in which one person exercises control over the other, even if it seems to have a noble purpose. For example, buying booze for your alcoholic spouse is not sacrificial or helpful; it's just as harmful as spoon-feeding sugar to your diabetic child. Giving in to every whim and desire of your spouse turns him or her into a self-centered brat, not a marital partner whose care and concern is focused on you.

Your altruistic self-giving may feel fulfilling for a while; it may lead to higher estimation in the eyes of your in-laws (who are secretly glad that you took their problem off their hands). Sadly, extreme self-sacrifice leads to depletion, not fulfillment. Its ugly results are disappointment, anger, and resentment, which can "leak out"—on your spouse, and also on others. In the long run, "holding nothing back" is self-destructive and not recommended as the path to a successful union.

Marriage is a two-way street, not a one-way rescue mission.

PARTING THOUGHT

"Before marriage, a man declares that he would lay down his life to serve you; after marriage, he won't even lay down his newspaper to talk to you."[1]

FOR FURTHER REFLECTION

What personal needs and desires have you set aside for the sake of your partner? How much would feel like too much?

What personal needs and desires has your partner set aside for your sake? How much is it reasonable for you to expect?

Do you think that your spouse takes advantage of you? How do you feel when that happens? How do you address that situation with your partner?

1. Rowland, "So Feminine," 53.

Seeking Your Perfect Partner for Your Perfect Marriage

Once you have figured out what your fantasy marriage will be, the search begins. It starts at all different times for people—as early as pre-adolescence for some, through adolescence, during college, or early career for many others. But it may not stop if you still have no partner, or you're shopping for a spouse due to a divorce or the death of your partner. You may even arrive at your golden years and be looking for someone to ease your loneliness.

What are you looking for? What are the traits of the right person for you? How do you pick and choose from the hundreds of millions of people inhabiting this planet at any one moment?

Your search will be guided by your beliefs and expectations about marriage. Whether you are aware of them or not, your search and success will also be influenced by the guiding principles that you are using for your selection. Who to date and who not? How long should you stay before you jump ship? What is a "passing grade" for the person who will win the lottery and get to marry you?

PARTING THOUGHT

"All too often people concentrate on finding the right spouse, little realizing that half of any marriage is being the right spouse."[1]

---

1. Qadhi, AZ Quotes.

7

There's Only One Perfect Person in the World Meant Just for You

MYTHICAL THINKING

There is an unnamed power at work in the universe, and let's call this force "the Matchmaker." The Matchmaker has only one purpose—to help you find and make the connection to the person you should marry. This is a huge responsibility because the Matchmaker already knows the exact person who is your destiny. Out of all the billions of people in the world, and all the languages that are spoken, you must be in exactly the right place and at precisely the right time so that you can cross paths with your future spouse.

Although there seems to be no room for error, in fact the Matchmaker often falls asleep at the switch and otherwise misses the mark, which explains the number of divorces in the world. People still believe in the Matchmaker, though, and give the Matchmaker another chance to set up an encounter with your "one and only."

For some people, the power of the Matchmaker is almost god-like, because they are waiting to find their "soulmate," the match that is "made in heaven."

For others, their belief in the Matchmaker is not strong enough. They do not believe that their spouse is "the perfect one." So even though they are married, they keep looking, always believing that there is "someone better out there." They believe that sooner or later the truly "right person" will be found, with or without the help of the Matchmaker.

In case you don't know, the Matchmaker lives at an undisclosed site called the CAFÉ (the Center for Amazing and Fantastic Extroverts) with other impossibly wonderful creatures who perform special deeds throughout the universe. Residents of the CAFÉ include the Easter Bunny, the Tooth Fairy, the Great Pumpkin, Grandfather Frost, and Mr. and Mrs. Claus and their elves.

This belief is so strong because the reward is so great. The Perfect Partner will fulfill all your needs and desires. The Spot-On Spouse will satisfy you in every way, leading to total happiness and marital paradise. Being matched with the perfect person is definitely worth waiting for!

ON SECOND THOUGHT . . .

The myth of a Matchmaker seems to be of special appeal to "people of faith." They passively wait for God to drop the Perfect Partner into their laps, or into their dating apps. This belief is attractive because it's supposed to make their life easier. They are relieved of taking any responsibility or making any effort to find someone with whom they are willing to foster a healthy long-term relationship.

Of course, this belief actually makes their life harder because (spoiler alert) there is no such place as the CAFÉ. One day each of you must face the reality that no one lives at the CAFÉ. Accepting that reality leads to disappointment and sorrow. Accepting that reality also opens a space for a new belief—that in this world today there are lots of people with whom you can create and develop a marital partnership; and that you are responsible for your own growth and nurturing your partner because neither of you is perfect.

PARTING THOUGHT

"Marriages are made in heaven. Then again, so are thunder, lightning, tornadoes, and hail."[1]

FOR FURTHER REFLECTION

Do you believe in Destiny, and looking for the Perfect Partner?

What does dating feel like when you are searching for the Spot-On Spouse?

Do you have some criteria for when you will stop your search, and then what you will do?

1. Unknown.

8

Your Spouse Should Be Able to Read Your Mind and Know What You Want and Need

MYTHICAL THINKING

Because someone loves you, they will naturally know you very well, and that's what you should expect. Your beloved should know you inside and out, and therefore know at any moment what you want and need. That person should be so attuned to you that your wants and needs are known by them before you yourself are conscious of them. This is a powerful skill known as "mind-reading."

You shouldn't have to *ask* for something because a good partner will already know what you want. You shouldn't have to *wait* for anything, because a spouse worthy of you will be ready with it at the time you need it. If you have to ask for it, then it's not worth the effort. A suitable partner will always be tuned into your feelings and instinctively know exactly how to respond to you. It's like they are in your head—in a really good way!

It is also important to clarify early in your relationship your wants and needs are the same thing. If you want something, then you do need it. So resist any efforts to separate these into two categories, as if you should expect not to get everything that you want.

This is a very important aptitude for your partner to have. As a skilled mind-reader your spouse will be properly equipped to keep you happy at all times by knowing *what* you want and need and precisely *when* it should be given to you.

This is definitely one of the character traits you should look for in a potential spouse before you decide to wed in order to have a thoroughly happy and satisfying marriage

ON SECOND THOUGHT . . .

Be forewarned! This trait comes back to bite you in the butt because

a. Later on you will get frustrated because your spouse thinks they can read your mind!

b. Your spouse will also expect the same of you—you should be able to read their mind. You should *know* what they want and need without ever having to tell you.

c. Your spouse will later get frustrated with you for thinking that you can read their mind.

These warnings are brought to you by the Association of Failed Mind-readers. The AFM asserts that spouses have to learn how to ask one another for what they want and need. They also need to inquire whether their response has been helpful.

Members of the AFM have become very wary of relying on their assumptions and presumptions. They learned the hard way (and have the scars to prove it) that it seemed easier to act on the assumption than to check it out first. They learned the hard way that presumptions based on past experience might not be true in the present moment, and it's more respectful (and safer) to ask rather than gamble that their presumption is right. Assumptions and presumptions are like grenades that can blow up in your face.

Alas, it also turns out that dictionaries insist that wants and needs are not the same thing. Go figure! Your *needs* are necessary; they are essential. There are serious consequences, including death, if needs are not met. Food is a need; water is a need; a Maserati is not a need. A healthy body is a need; coloring your hair is not a need.

Your *wants* are your desires; they give you pleasure. Despite your feelings, there are not serious consequences when you don't get something you *want* (disappointment, anger, and sadness are not life-threatening, just uncomfortable).

When you accept the difference between your wants and needs, you can avoid a fair amount of disappointment, anger, and sadness about not getting something you wanted. You also have more motivation to ask for both your needs and wants. It increases the chances you will get them (better odds than waiting for your spouse to read your mind). You will also realize that you won't always get everything you want. And that your spouse may not be the only person in a position to give you what you want or need (which will take a big burden off their shoulders).

Please remember, your spouse also expects you to be a superb mind-reader, and will be filled with disappointment, resentment, and anger when you don't figure it out . . . Except for the times they get mad because you thought you had it figured out, but got it wrong!

It turns out mind-reading isn't all it's cracked up to be.

PARTING THOUGHT

"Great relationships are based on clarity, not mind-reading."[1]

FOR FURTHER REFLECTION

When did you first learn to read other people's mind? How good are you? Does your spouse agree with that assessment?

1. Arterburn, *AZ Quotes*.

Does your partner also possess the skill of mind-reading? Are they good at it? How do you feel when they try and misread you?

How well do you communicate your wants, needs, and preferences? How are those communications received? What could be done to improve the communication?

9

The History of Your Partner's Relationships Doesn't Matter

MYTHICAL THINKING

Dating and courtship are exciting because of the adventure of meeting a new person. It's like a gift package waiting to be opened. Of course, you know by now that a gift you receive might not be the "perfect gift," but it's still fun to receive a present and find out what's inside.

Speed dating intensifies that excitement by allowing you to open a bunch of presents in one afternoon or evening: "Number six seems great and is someone I'd like to date. I want to get to know number three better. Number eight and I really seemed to click." Everything seems fresh and new and thrilling.

There's more excitement as you spend time together, share activities, and get to know each other better. It's easy to slide over the little tidbits that tumble out—your future father-in-law is actively alcoholic (but that's OK because he still holds a good job); she was engaged three times (but that doesn't matter because the groom always left before the wedding); he has a great work history (he holds each job for six months and then quits to find a better one); the future in-laws sometimes get physical during a heated argument (it's not that bad—only twice did someone have to go to the ER); your future spouse was in jail for six months for breaking and entering (because the court did not understand the extenuating circumstances, and the lawyer was lousy); and yes, you have declared bankruptcy twice (but it's not as bad as it sounds; it just means you can't get a credit card, a car loan, or a mortgage for several years).

ON SECOND THOUGHT . . .

Getting to know someone can be invigorating. Here's the dilemma: the relationship is new and fresh, but *you* are not new and fresh, and neither is the person you're dating.

Each of you brings your whole history into that new relationship (infancy, childhood, adolescence and young adulthood). Each of you brings your family of origin with all of their blessings and letdowns. Each of you brings your cultural, ethnic, and perhaps religious background. Each of you brings your medical history. Each of you brings your educational and employment history. Each of you brings your circle of friends, be it large or small. Each of you brings your history of dating relationships, which may be limited or extensive, with its successes and failures as well as your expectations and assumptions.

Each of you is a wonderful collection of all these things and much more. They don't disappear or even fade into the background when you start a new relationship. You don't come into a new relationship "with a blank slate." More likely your slate has a lot of smudges and erasures and re-writes.

The idea that they don't mean anything may be wishful thinking so you don't have to deal with whatever makes you uncomfortable. However, all of that history is significant information because our behavior tends to be consistent throughout our relationships.

The histories of you and your potential partner cannot be ignored or swept under the rug. They affect you and make you the person you are today. Pay attention to them because they will affect the course of your relationship in the weeks and years ahead of you.

PARTING THOUGHT

"The past is not dead—it isn't even past."[1]

FOR FURTHER REFLECTION

What is in your background that you're inclined to hold back? What about in your family?

How do you think your life experiences might affect your long-term relationship?

When's a good time to disclose painful or embarrassing information that you'd rather not share? Is there a good way to do that?

1. Wolf, *Patterns of Childhood.*

10

Living Together before Marriage Always Increases Your Chance of a Successful Marriage

MYTHICAL THINKING

It seems to make sense that a marriage is more likely to be successful if you get some experience tucked under your belt. So living with someone will help you to know what that's like. Getting to know a potential spouse better is a positive goal. If you live together for a while, there will be time to get to know their friends and their family too. Getting some sexual practice will remove some bumbling, fear, and tension later on (see Myth 32). All of these things will help the two of you to lay down a strong foundation for a long and happy marriage.

ON SECOND THOUGHT . . .

The research about American couples, cohabitation, and marriage has been compiled for several decades. The idea that premarital cohabitation is associated with better outcomes in marriage is *not* supported by the research.

In fact, premarital cohabitation is associated with poorer marriage *stability*, meaning that couples who cohabited had a lower rate of staying married compared to those who did not live together.

There is also a poorer marriage *quality* (i.e., satisfaction, adjustment, and overall happiness) for those who cohabited, though the negative effect is not as strong as it is on marriage stability. There is also a substantial amount of research which underlines the detrimental role of cohabitation on the well-being of children.

There are two nuances to note from this research. The negative impact is especially true for people who have cohabited multiple times without expecting it to lead to marriage. In the long term they manifest lower marital stability and lower marriage quality, and they show lower regard for the institution of marriage.

Second, there is an exception. Engaged couples who cohabit for a brief period of time before their wedding show no significant difference in their marital stability and marital quality when compared to couples who did not cohabit before marriage.

Therefore, cohabiting for the sake of getting some experience has negative results rather than the hoped for positive results of creating and strengthening a long-term marriage. Sorry, folks.

Your goals are worthwhile goals. The good news is that you can accomplish most of your goals without cohabitation. You can have roommates and housemates in college and early years of employment. You can learn how to live with others, and hone your skills of working through stress and disagreements. You can take time to get to know your prospective spouse without living together (and there is less strain because you have time to be separate, reflect, and adjust). You can find out the differences between things that are an annoyance and things that are "deal-breakers." You can "make haste slowly," taking more time to get to know your potential partner's family and friends (see Myth 10).

There are things you can do to help create a healthy marriage. "Practicing marriage" by cohabiting is not necessarily one of them.[1]

PARTING THOUGHT

"Not cohabitation but consensus institutes marriage."[2]

FOR FURTHER REFLECTION

If cohabiting is an option you'd consider, what reasons would support your decision to cohabit?

What specific relationship skills do you want to have when you're married? Are there ways you can learn and improve those skills without living together with a potential spouse?

What are some relationship traits or behaviors that you would like to diminish or be rid of when you're married? What can you do about them now instead of waiting until "some time" in the future?

1. Our thanks to Dr. Gary Bischof at Western Michigan University who collected and summarized research about cohabitation and marriage.

2. Cicero, *AZ Quotes*

11

Every Irritating Behavior of Your Partner Disappears after the Wedding

MYTHICAL THINKING

Do you remember that wonderful period of time while you were dating when your new friend was faultless? There was nothing that spoiled that unique and spectacular combination of beauty, intelligence, sense of humor, athletic ability, and special talents. You almost had to wonder how time had passed and that this incredible person had not yet been snatched up.

And then one day, they farted, or snorted, or told a joke that was just plain stupid, or you found out they liked a food that you can't stand, or they hated your favorite movie (how could *anyone* possibly hate that movie?!). The image was tarnished; the light dimmed.

You were able to stick it out, though, because of one important piece of information you held in your back pocket—you knew that once the wedding took place, all those things would disappear. The deep love for one another that both of you expressed publicly before your family and friends would also be the occasion for a miracle (a wedding gift that your spouse needed the most!)

ON SECOND THOUGHT . . .

During the time of your dating, courtship, and engagement, you're bound to bump into some things that irritate you. Some of them may have delighted you at one time, and now they grate on you every time they occur. Once you notice these annoying habits and behaviors, you find that it's very hard to ignore them—they're like fingernails on the blackboard of your brain.

Weddings are a great way to celebrate the wonderful partner you have discovered and to whom you want to make a personal commitment. Planning a wedding is often an exercise in trying to make dreams come true: "I've always dreamed that my wedding . . ." And maybe you'll be fortunate enough that some of those dreams come true.

But a wedding does not unleash magical powers for newlyweds. The person who witnesses your vows is not a magician and no magic wand is used during the ceremony. The officiant possesses no secret strength to change you or your spouse now that you are husband and wife. Neither of you is a sleeping beauty or a prince with life-changing power in your lips; a kiss is just a kiss.

(Be careful about finding Prince Charming; it turns out he was a compulsive womanizer who married Sleeping Beauty, Snow White, and Cinderella.)

In some way it may seem that everything has changed, but in other ways, that's not so. You are the same person the day before your wedding and the day after, and the same is true about your new spouse. Nothing magical happens at the ceremony or during your wedding night which provokes an immediate and profound transformation in your spouse when all their bad habits and irritating character traits miraculously disappear.

PARTING THOUGHT

"I love being married. It's so great to find that one special person you want to annoy for the rest of your life."[1]

1. Rudner, *AZ Quotes.*

FOR FURTHER REFLECTION

Do you remember a moment with someone significant in your life when you were shocked to discover that they were not perfect? What did you see or hear or find out, and how did that change your perception and thoughts about that person? How might this apply to your future spouse?

Do you believe in the magical powers of a wedding—that a ceremony will miraculously make things change? Where did that belief come from?

If you have already celebrated your wedding, did you have any expectation of what would be different after that event? In reality, how did things change? Were there any significant surprises?

12

Your Love Is So Powerful That You Can Change Your Partner after You Get Married

MYTHICAL THINKING

Falling in love might be one of the greatest experiences in the whole world. You understand why people can't keep the news to themselves, why they talk about it, write songs and poems and make movies about it. It feels soooooooo goooood; it's exhilarating. It is so empowering that it sets you free from a lack of self-confidence; it helps you believe that you *can* do things that you never thought possible.

The power of love which you possess is so powerful that you can actually use it to change your spouse. That power switch gets turned on at your wedding, and from that time forward, you have a personal power that can make your spouse's bad habits and annoying mannerisms disappear. Note: you have to wait until after the wedding to exercise this power; you already know it has no effect during the courtship or engagement period.

Sometimes the power of love operates in a subversive manner. Your spouse can believe that the impulse to drop those habits and desire to stop those irritating behaviors came from within because *their* love for you is so strong. (But you know where it really came from—you!). Your other-half at this point has not evolved enough to be your better-half, and truth be told, likely never will. But you are there to help them get close.

This power may also manifest itself through what some people think is prayer. Such people are so convinced of their personal wisdom and insight that they can convince God to take the necessary actions to fix a spouse. A faith-filled partner can "pray away" the spouse's problems, if they say the prayer properly and really truly believe.

ON SECOND THOUGHT . . .

Q. How many psychologists does it take to change a light bulb?
A. Only one, but the light bulb has to want to be changed.

Sorry to say, you might be able to change a light bulb, but you don't have the power to change another person, not even the one you love. No one has that much power, not even you. Lots of people try, though. You can make great efforts and devote years to your effort, believing that you have such power, or believing that your repeated prayers for your spouse can accomplish what your own powerful love cannot.

You can suggest changes.

Your spouse can deny your request.

You can lightly tease.

Your spouse can ignore you.

You can drop subtle hints.

Your spouse can not hear you.

You can drop immense hints.

Your spouse can resist.

You can push your spouse.

Your spouse can push back.

Here's what experience teaches us: your spouse's power to ignore and deny and resist is even stronger than your power of love.

Love does not conquer all.

PARTING THOUGHT

"The tragedy of marriage is that while all women marry thinking that their man will change, all men marry believing their wife will never change."[1]

FOR FURTHER REFLECTION

Who have you tried to change? How did it go? Has anybody tried to change you? Did you like it? Were they successful?

What are some times that you tried to change yourself? Did you establish your goal, the steps to reach your goal, and then jump right in and accomplish everything you set out to do? How did that go?

If you've had any experience of ignoring, delaying, or resisting, how did you move past that?

---

1. Deighton, *London Match*, 15.

13

Postpone Talking about Touchy Issues Because They Will Go Away after Your Wedding

MYTHICAL THINKING

Some couples spend their time getting to know each other better. When they run into some difference of opinion they may try to convince each other of their own position; then one of them gets enlightened, and they move on. They encounter some difficulty and then spend time exploring and listening to one another and seeking to understand the spouse's feeling and point of view. They negotiate a way forward that both of them can live with. Or they agree to accept the fact that, in this case, they will simply agree to disagree.

Oh my heavens! You can save yourself so much time and effort by remembering this one simple truth—all of that talking and listening and negotiating is a colossal waste of time because all those differences and difficulties will disappear as soon as you get married!

Your love and commitment to one another simply do not require you to take time for all that talking and listening and negotiating.

Now you understand why weddings are so stressful—there is so much that happens besides the ceremony and the reception. The universe is being filled with your newlywed-garbage—all your irritating behaviors are being swept away; your unresolved issues are being sucked into black holes and disappearing forever. And before you even depart for your honeymoon, each of you has been so transformed by the power of your love that you hardly recognize each other on your wedding night.

If for some reason this makeover did not occur at your wedding, you must immediately put into action these two sacred principles for dealing with your issues: Postponement and Procrastination. Do not wait to start procrastinating; begin immediately. Don't try to discuss things or resolve your problems. Set them aside for another day. Never put off till tomorrow what you can put off till the day after tomorrow. Later is always the better option, and the later the better.

ON SECOND THOUGHT . . .

If this behavior were a college class, it would be called Avoidance 101. Avoidance does not make difficult topics disappear; their heads are just below the surface of the water, watching carefully for a chance to pop out and say, "Boo!"

Or the real issues leak out masquerading as some other matter: "You left the top off the tube of toothpaste again" is just another way of complaining that you think your partner is a slob, and you're sick and tired of cleaning up their messes. And pointing out that "You're more concerned about the toothpaste than you are about me," is just another way of saying "You're a compulsive neatnik and I'm here to tell you that dust is not a contagious life-threatening disease."

When couples run into a difference of opinion they can try to convince each other of their own position; then if one of them gets enlightened, they can move on. On other occasions they can encounter a difficulty and then spend time exploring and listening to one another and seeking to understand the spouse's feeling and point of view. Then they negotiate a way forward that both of them can live with. Or they agree to accept the fact that, in this case, they will simply agree to disagree.

Avoidance does not make disagreements disappear. They just sit around until it's time to make another awkward appearance.

PARTING THOUGHT

"Avoidance doesn't solve anything; it only serves as a temporary salve."[1]

FOR FURTHER REFLECTION

Can you name some difficult or emotional issues that your partner prefers to postpone, procrastinate, and delay dealing with? What techniques are used for avoidance? What happens when you try to bring them up?

Can you name some difficult or emotional issues that you prefer to postpone, procrastinate, and delay dealing with? What are your preferred techniques? Does your partner know about these issues and these techniques? What do you do when your partner tries to address those issues?

What do you gain by avoidance? What problems are caused by your avoidance? Can you name some ways that your avoidance "leaks out" and causes problems?

1. Dungy, *Uncommon*, 160.

14

If Something Goes Wrong at the Wedding Ceremony, Your Marriage Will Fail

MYTHICAL THINKING

Any problem at the wedding is an omen that the marriage is not meant to be.

The practical implication of this is that the wedding has to go perfectly in order to avoid even the possibility of a glitch.

Another practical implication is that you must plan everything down to the last detail. Your schedule requires military precision. Your clothes must fit perfectly and be without a crease. The reception must be flawless—including the decorations, a cake, a menu (suitable for carnivores, vegans, dieters, and overeaters), seating, music, waitstaff, guests, DJ, wedding party, first dance(s), eloquent speeches, and favors for the guests.

You must consult many bridal magazines and websites to find out what you are still missing. You must also incorporate all the suggestions you receive from your family, your in-laws, your cousins, your wedding party, and a multitude of helpful friends "who saw this once at a wedding and thought it was great!" You must manage the crushing disappointment of all the people whose suggestions you just couldn't fit into one wedding despite your best efforts.

As the day gets closer, you wish the whole thing were over—and the wedding hasn't even happened yet!

Then comes the Big Day—and all day long you are anxious and stressed, concerned that all your planning is implemented and that all your efforts were not wasted. Then something happens, and (internally) you collapse into a heap because things did not go as you planned:

you accidently blow out the flame of your marriage candle;

someone may become ill or couldn't come at the last minute (the maid of honor delivered a baby after the rehearsal dinner; the groom was stung by a bee on the second joint of his ring finger);

something interrupts the ceremony (the flower girl refuses to walk down the aisle and instead decides to scream bloody murder in the vestibule).[1]

At that very moment your wedding drops from the heights of pure joy to the hellish abyss of embarrassment, and horror. You must keep smiling, while there's a voice screaming in your ear, "What will people think?!" And your brain is sending out a repeating message: "My wedding is ruined! We haven't even finished the wedding and there are already problems; it's obvious my marriage is doomed."

Oh, happy day! Yet many newlyweds have said that they barely remember the day. Many newlyweds have said they barely remember the day, despite their efforts to make it memorable.

---

1. These are all true incidents at weddings at which I presided.

ON SECOND THOUGHT . . .

There are lots and lots of "pieces in a wedding-puzzle." There are so many people involved in a series of events including a rehearsal, rehearsal dinner, wedding, reception, maybe another gathering the next day, and a honeymoon; plus transportation from one place to the next for a bunch of people. What do you really think are the odds that it's going to go without a hitch? What odds would they give you in Las Vegas that you can manage all those pieces and pull off a "perfect wedding?"

It might be helpful to recall what is actually required for a wedding—a license, a bride and groom, an official witness (clergy or civil official), and two witnesses who can verify they saw it.

Everything else is extra. Instead of a list of all the things you "have to do," you might start with the legal requirements, and then decide what extras you want to add.

Another approach is to select a few words to guide your planning. What is it that you want people to remember about the day? What do you want the day to be like—festive, serious, joyful, prayerful? Do you have a particular image, such as "family day," or "incredible food," that you would like to characterize your wedding day? Then you can use those select words or images to guide your decisions—does X fit that image, or can you let it go? Does Y serve your purpose well, or is it an unneeded extra?

Make some choices; do some planning; and create some good memories. Don't set yourself up for a wedding day of dread, anxiety, and fear of what can go wrong, and don't keep a list of things that didn't go as you planned (which, by the way, often make the best memories).

PARTING THOUGHT

"More marriages might survive if the partners realized that sometimes the better comes after the worse."[2]

2. Larson, *AZ Quotes*.

FOR FURTHER REFLECTION

How stressed were you on your wedding day? Did your wedding and reception go perfectly? Are there things that make you laugh now, or feel sad? Did people enjoy themselves that day?

Can you make any direct connections between events on the day you married and how that adversely affected your marital relationship?

What advice would you give to engaged couples about planning a wedding?

Living Your "Dream Marriage"

Congratulations! You made it! You found and married the perfect spouse!! Despite all the nay-sayers, and all the cautions raised by this book, you managed to work the marriage algorithm, defied the odds, and snagged your one and only true love!!! Forever and ever!!!!

Now you just have to preserve this perfect union for years, decades, and with health care advances, maybe a century. That is a lot of living, and a lot of loving. Is it possible your relationship will change at some point? Will the state of nirvana at the beginning of your union last for your whole life?

Building a foundation is important so that your perfect union will endure. So let's not waste any time. You need to get going, and find out what you have to do to make this miracle last.

PARTING THOUGHT

"Marriage has no guarantees. If that's what you're looking for, go live with a car battery."[1]

---

1. Bombeck, *AZ Quotes.*

15

Stability Should Be
the Highest Priority of a Marriage

MYTHICAL THINKING

Once the wedding is over, everything in your relationship will settle into blissful steadiness. There are no surprises, only the rock-solid strength of two-who-are-one.

This is the reason that one of the biggest threats to a happy marriage is Change (and that doesn't mean the coins in your pocket).

Change should be avoided at all costs—you don't want your partner to change; and you yourself certainly don't want to change. Do your very best to keep everything exactly as it was on the first day of your marriage, your perfect wedding day (see Myths 11–13).

Do everything you can to prevent yourself and your partner from changing.

Avoidance is the first principle. Do not talk about Change. Do not even think about it. Change is dangerous; de-stabilizing; upsetting; and has nothing good to offer you.

Postponing and procrastination are also good principles for dealing with this threat (see Myth 13). You can postpone anything that your spouse wants to do that's new or different. You can also procrastinate by dragging your feet and putting off (forever) any wild and crazy idea that pops into your head about making some tiny adjustment. As if such a thing might be helpful or productive.

Be careful, because Change is sneaky. You may agree to what you think is just a little bitty modification, or you alter something with a promise that it will be an improvement, or you try something that you believe your partner won't even notice, but then Change has got its foot in the door. Danger! It's best to keep that door closed, sealed, and triple padlocked.

Change is also seductive. It holds out beautiful promises, telling you how much better things can be than what they are already. These are lies! You already have a perfect marriage, so what could possibly improve? Nothing! There is no need for Change. Absolutely none!

Stagnation is a true sign of a healthy relationship.

ON SECOND THOUGHT . . .

You only have to look at your body to realize that no one stays the same—newborn, infant, toddler, child, adolescent, young adult, middle-aged adult, senior. How can we possibly entertain the notion that two people who are changing everyday could create a union that does not and must not change? Change is inevitable.

You can also make choices that influence and direct how those changes may occur. For your body you can exercise, overeat, be active, or be a couch potato. Couples can discuss ideas or act in secret. They can be partners who plan together, or behave like single people who only act independently. They can be supportive of one another when making changes, or be derogatory of those attempts by tossing ridicule and sarcasm at each other.

Here's an amazing thing. Some people can hold two or more myths at the same time. So while you may believe that any change is dangerous because it puts your marriage at risk, at the same time you also may believe that it's important to help your partner "grow" into what you want them to be, using whatever means are necessary. This means that you can have the best of both worlds—a totally stable marriage, and a new and improved spouse!

If you are the same couple after four years of marriage and forty-four years of marriage, then you have wasted forty years. A wedding is simply the kickoff for a great adventure of exploring, growing, improving, failing at times, and starting again, getting better and better with age, just like a good wine.

No marriage stays the same, and stagnation is nothing to aspire to.

PARTING THOUGHT

"Marriage is not a static state between two unchanging people. Marriage is a psychological and spiritual journey that begins in the ecstasy of attraction, meanders through a rocky stretch of self-discovery, and culminates in the creation of an intimate, joyful, lifelong union."[1]

FOR FURTHER REFLECTION

What are some changes you have made in your life that you're proud of?

What in your marriage do you never want to change? What in your marriage do you want to improve?

How do you respond when your spouse suggests a change (a new recipe? rearranging the furniture? a different vacation?) How do you respond when your partner wants to change something that you thought was already decided?

1. Hendrix, *Getting the Love You Want*, 42.

16

Always Expect to Do Family Rituals the Way Your Family Did

MYTHICAL THINKING

You come from a family, and your family had rituals. Whether or not you called them rituals doesn't matter. Your family had patterns of behavior, prescribed ways of doing things. For example, how did you celebrate birthdays—did the whole family show up, or did the day pass unnoticed? Were there gifts, no gifts; cards, cards with money, never cards with money? Do you rip off the wrapping paper, or carefully remove it and save it for the next time? How did you celebrate Christmas—dinner the night before or on Christmas day, and what was the expected menu? Did you go to Church and, if so, when? When did the tree go up and get taken down? What did you do for New Year's Eve? Juneteenth? Thanksgiving? Hanukkah?

So when you're married, that's how things will be done—the way your family did. For example, when your spouse is excited about a new recipe, it's really helpful to say, "My mother made it better."

This discrepancy of assumptions about how you will celebrate family rituals can be quite exciting as the two of you engage in a struggle to make these important decisions. The one who wins is clearly the better and smarter spouse. This is the time to stick up for your family so "things are done right!"

The way your partner's family did things doesn't really matter much in the scheme of things (although perhaps your partner doesn't see it that way). However, you may encounter just a little pushback from your spouse who believes exactly the same way you do—that things must be done right, and where did your family come up with such weird ideas anyway?

Along with all that, you must figure out not only *what* you'll do for each occasion, and also *where* you'll do them—at home? with your family? with your in-laws? at a restaurant?

Finally, these happy occasions have another layer—who do you love more? Because if you win, it becomes clear to your spouse that you love your family of origin more than you love your spouse. So by all means, do your best to win so that things can be done right!

ON SECOND THOUGHT . . .

As equal partners in a marriage, it's a mistaken but commonly accepted notion that things will be done *your* way. That includes family rituals.

Rituals are significant part of the culture of marriage and family—they add richness to the fabric of a couple and a family. It's important that you find ways to mark significant occasions, be they holidays, personal achievements, or ways to respond to illness and death.

If you refer to Myth 22, you'll see that this does not have to be a winner-takes-all decision. There are several options: what your family did, and what your partner's family did, are the two most obvious. You can also take turns and switch back and forth from year to year.

You can also create your own family rituals (and have fun doing it!) Be adventurous, and make some new traditions of your own.

PARTING THOUGHT

"Real giving is when we give to our spouses what's important to them, whether we understand it, like it, agree with it, or not."[1]

FOR FURTHER REFLECTION

What rituals have you incorporated that came from your spouse or their family?

If given the chance, are there any family rituals from your childhood you would change, drop, or add? Can you explain why?

If you wanted to be more creative, how would you re-design some of your family rituals?

---

1. Davis, *The Divorce Remedy,* 54.

17

There Is No Place for Joy and Laughter in Marriage; It's All Serious Work

MYTHICAL THINKING . . .

In light of your commitment, you have the right and the duty to set out clear expectations for your spouse. Your partner needs to be clear about the do's and don'ts in your marriage. You may have promised "for better or worse," but there's really no room in your relationship for "worse." Life should only be headed in one direction, and that toward "better," which calls for constant improvement with clear goals and objectives.

You must be relentless. Do not allow slack. Maintain pressure. Leisure is just a waste of time. Keep working in order to surpass your targets. Stability is for wimps (see Myth 15). You are an achiever!

One of the ways to keep your marriage serious is to set really high standards. Do not be realistic about the human condition—expect your partner to be a living saint, one who aspires to be as good as you are already.

Keep the anxiety level up! Maintain a constant level of worry and fear about whether your marriage is working. Keep a running list of things that might possibly go wrong, and worry about those things too. (Worrying about them stops them from happening).

ON SECOND THOUGHT . . .

It's not very appealing to hear someone say, "I'm working on my marriage." Effort is one thing; work is another. Marriage is not a task. Marriage is not a job for which you collect wages and benefits at the end of the week.

Marriage is not a work relationship and you are not your spouse's supervisor. You do not set goals and objectives, and you do not evaluate how your spouse is doing based on your personal standards and expectations. Nor are you your partner's coach or teacher.

Marriage is a partnership. Partners stand shoulder to shoulder and hip to hip. They face the future together and walk into it side by side.

As a spouse you can do some roleplaying! You can be a lover, a cheerleader, a colleague, a friend, a supporter, and a source of encouragement. It is important that your focus is not to look for the deficits of your spouse with a disclaimer that "I'm just trying to help you."

When you're tempted to raise the standards, remember that the saints were not easy to live with. Lighten up, and enjoy your marriage.

Not so seriously speaking—Did you know that 85 percent of marriage consists of a spouse yelling "What?" from another part of the house?

You'll know you've been married a long time when your spouse asks you to strip—only because your spouse wants to fill empty space in the washing machine.

An elderly couple who had been married for decades went to a new restaurant. The waiter noticed that all during the meal the husband spoke to his wife with a variety of endearments—my treasure, my sweetness, my deepest love. When the wife excused herself for a moment, the waiter commented, "Wow! After all these years, you still use such lovely words with your wife." And he responded, "Actually, I forgot her name about three years ago."

PARTING THOUGHT

"There is such pleasure in long-term marriage that I really would hate to be my age and not have had a long-term marriage. Remember, sustaining a pleasurable, long-term marriage takes effort, deliberateness, and an intention to learn about one another. In other words, marriage is for grown-ups."[1]

FOR FURTHER REFLECTION

What are some things that make you laugh in your marriage? What are some memories that still bring a smile to your face when you remember them?

Can you name some things you do that make you laugh at yourself?

What are some areas of your relationship in which it could be helpful to lighten up?

1. Roberts, *AZ Quotes*.

18

Make Sure to Hide Your Fears and Weaknesses from Your Spouse

MYTHICAL THINKING

From the beginning of your relationship this is an important behavior pattern to establish. When you are first getting to know each other, the last thing you want to do is disclose something that makes you look less desirable. As the relationship progresses, you realize the need to exercise caution and say nothing so you don't mess up something that's going well. As the relationship gets deeper and more intense, you know that there's a great risk that comes with any big revelation, so it's best to keep quiet. And by the time you're engaged and married, it's hard to imagine exposing any new significant information. So the silence must persist, and the hiding must continue.

It makes sense to keep things hidden—it helps you not to look like an inferior or flawed person. If there's something bad in your past, your partner might conclude you are a thoroughly bad person and run in the opposite direction. You don't want your partner to discover that you are a donkey or an outright idiot.

As time goes on, you can convince yourself that those things are buried so well that chances are your spouse will never notice them—unless they google your name on the internet, and then who knows what will be found?

The risk of revealing something seems to get bigger and bigger with time, the potential consequences loom larger, and the soft decision to "wait until later" becomes a decision hard as concrete to "never tell." Because if your spouse finds out you have a weakness of some kind, the whole marriage may go down the tubes.

ON SECOND THOUGHT . . .

What better person to share your vulnerability with than the person who cares about you so deeply that they joined their life to yours?

How can your partner support you, encourage you, and comfort you if you do not divulge what you need?

Hiding is destructive, and it deprives you of the opportunity to receive what your spouse has to give. Hiding suggests that there is a lack of trust in your relationship.

And what do you suppose your partner will think, then feel, and how will they react when they do find out—not only *what* you have hidden, but also that you made the decision to *hide* it in the first place?

It's a delusion that your spouse will not realize that you are vulnerable in some ways, because in all likelihood your spouse already knows about your weaknesses, and can point out a few more that you haven't recognized or admitted to yourself.

It's just like failing to change the oil in your car—the longer you go, the worse it gets. Hiding for a longer time is not what saves a marriage but what damages it.

PARTING THOUGHT

"People do not marry people, not real ones anyway; they marry what they think the person is; they marry illusions and images. The exciting adventure of marriage is finding out who the partner really is."[1]

FOR FURTHER REFLECTION

Are there some things you are hiding from your spouse? Can you be honest with yourself about why you're doing that (see myth 2)?

Can you be honest with yourself first of all, about your own weaknesses, limitations, fears, and vulnerabilities? Are they really as bad as you think they are?

What kind of circumstances can you create to help you have a discussion with your spouse about these things and feel safe doing so?

1. Framo, *Marital and Family Therapy.*

19

Love Conquers All and
Will Keep You Together

MYTHICAL THINKING

You have stumbled into something that many people do not know.
You have discovered that love is a powerful force. It makes you feel
like you can do things that you never believed were possible.

This is a slightly paraphrased quotation from paleontologist
Teilhard de Chardin, who also was a Jesuit priest who believed in
the power of love:

> Someday, after mastering the winds, the waves, the tides,
> and gravity, we shall harness the energy of love. And
> then, for the second time in world history—humanity
> will have discovered fire.[1]

Married couples for centuries have done this. You know that
you have received a magnificent, life-giving, and powerful gift
called love. It makes you very different from other couples, because you really love each other. Other people may not see it, but

---

1. Teilhard de Chardin, "Evolution of Chastity," 86–87.

you know the truth of this in your gut. You are doing your best to harness the energy of love.

You are a true believer in the power of your love. Therefore, you know that you will never have problems in your relationship because you are different than other couples. Your love will push all difficulties far away from you—because you *really* love each other. You said so at your wedding and you meant it. Your love is so powerful that it can ward off all demons, dangers, threats, and hazards that could harm your relationship in any way. It has wrapped you in a cocoon that is stronger and more protective than any force shield. Love will keep you together forever.

ON SECOND THOUGHT . . .

Love *is* a powerful force. It is enough to compel people to make great sacrifices, and to do heroic deeds. It is enough to make some people put their life on the line.

Love also feels great. It feels so good that some people chase it from one relationship to another.

Love is more than an emotion; it is also more than a force. Neither the feeling of love nor the power of love by itself is sufficient to sustain a lifelong relationship.

Love is a way of life. Therefore, love is also a commitment—that when you don't feel like it, or when your energy is down, you will continue to live a way of life that is loving. That kind of love takes effort; it doesn't just happen or carry on through sheer momentum.

That kind of love requires nurturing. It requires careful attention to sustain it—like caring for a prize orchid or a delicate bonsai tree. It takes effort to create an interpersonal environment for a healthy and satisfying long-term relationship. It takes personal effort to accommodate, to be flexible, to resolve conflict, and to deal with anger, jealousy, envy, and lust when they rear their fiery heads.

Love is not enough to wipe out the challenges of maintaining a strong relationship.

PARTING THOUGHT

"Love is an ideal thing, marriage a real thing; a confusion of the real with the ideal never goes unpunished."[2]

FOR FURTHER REFLECTION

What kinds of things interfere with your ability and willingness to love? How have you learned to overcome them?

Does your love feel as strong today as the memory of it on the day you married? What has strengthened that power? What has diminished it? What has injured that power? What has healed it?

What other things help you sustain your marital commitment besides the feeling of love?

---

2. von Goethe, *AZ Quotes*.

20

Men and Women Are from Different Planets

MYTHICAL THINKING

Men and women are very different, and we're talking about more than body parts. They see life so differently than the opposite sex that it's as if they come from different planets; sometimes it seems they may be living in different galaxies. They are not able to understand each other because their brains are wired so differently. It's so hard to imagine them living together in a harmonious fashion that the chances of a happy marriage range from unlikely to impossible.

For example, everyone knows that women are too emotional. They are also illogical (although a better word is irrational). Therefore women are constitutionally incapable of handling conflict and problem-solving. They use crying and "alligator tears" to get their way.

Everyone also knows that men don't have an emotional bone in their body (perhaps they were located in the rib that was removed from Adam to create Eve). Just mention "feelings" in front of men and you can see their eyes roll and their brains shut down as they shrink into their seat.

Actually, men are not biologically "built" for marriage. At their core they are Neanderthals, brutes who have to be strong and in control all the time. They must spread their seed everywhere in order to preserve the human race. Therefore, men are constitutionally incapable of being faithful to a partner. Monogamy is impossible for men.

There are other traits that everyone knows are feminine or masculine. It is important to teach your children what those are so that there's no confusion later on—you don't want them to grow up with some characteristic that obviously belongs to the other sex.

Acknowledging your gender differences sooner rather than later can help you to lower your expectations to zero (or maybe a one or two if you found a really good partner). If you did, by some pure chance, stumble on a mate who has evolved a bit, be sure to check out whether they have any traits that actually belong to the opposite sex.

In conclusion, it's impossible for men and women to get along, so why even bother to try. Make your peace with having a relationship with someone who shares household expenses, reduces your income tax (sometimes), and makes it more convenient to have sex once in a while, and forget about the rest.

ON SECOND THOUGHT . . .

Misunderstanding and conflict are not only the result of biological differences. Blaming a woman for your problems "because she's a woman" makes no more sense than blaming a man for your problems "because he's a man." They are just excuses that try to avoid addressing the difficulties that occur in interpersonal relationships; they're not even limited to marriage.

Yes, there are some gender differences that are related to their response to stress—men tend physiologically to be more reactive to stress and take more time to recover. Men also tend to have more negative self-talk internally. On the other hand, women tend to recover more quickly after a stress-response, and move sooner toward soothing and more conciliatory thoughts.[1]

However, there are skills that fall into the range of adult behavior that men and women can learn and put into practice. These skills are not gender-specific or gender-restricted. For example, women and men can learn listening skills and empathy.

Men and women are different; *vive la différence*. But they are not *that* different, and they can learn to be respectful, learn to live with those differences, and even appreciate them.

PARTING THOUGHT

"Men and women are like two feet; they can help each other get ahead."[2]

FOR FURTHER REFLECTION

What do you know to be true about men, and about women? Are there any exceptions?

What are the characteristics that are specifically masculine or feminine? If there are exceptions, how do you explain them?

How do you behave and talk differently when you are with men and with women? What are some constructive ways to deal with any differences you encounter?

1. Gottman, *Seven Principles*, 38–39.
2. Fisher, *The First Sex*.

21

Conflict Will Take Care of Itself If You Wait Long Enough

MYTHICAL THINKING

This little gem is so helpful. If any difference or discord between the two of you appears on the horizon, you can sweep it under the rug. It goes away, and it will never come up again. Investing in a large sturdy broom that will last you for years is well worth the price. Just ignore the big lump in the middle of your living room carpet.

Learning to avoid disputes helps you to avoid another problem—your lack of skills to solve problems and find solutions. If you diligently avoid the conflicts, then you don't have to bother learning any skills for resolution. You just have to learn to walk around all the lumps in your carpet.

Last, and perhaps most important, avoiding conflict also helps you to avoid the uncomfortable feelings that come along with conflict. You won't have to deal with the anger, sadness, fear, disappointment, or resentment that are also hiding under your rug.

So in the end, you're batting 1.000. You avoid conflict; you avoid problem-solving; and you avoid cruddy feelings. Bravo!

ON SECOND THOUGHT . . .

Alas, conflict is inevitable unless you and your spouse are identical twins (see Myth 4). Disagreements will emerge because you are two different people with your own values, beliefs, and ways of doing things. Your marriage is healthy when you and your spouse know how to resolve differences, not because you don't have any, or because you learned how to avoid them (in which case the lumps in your living room carpet are more like landmines waiting to explode).

There's good news here: not all problems are resolvable, but with some effort and practice lots of them are. It's not even necessary to bat 1.000 for your marriage to thrive.

There's more good news: one notable feature of conflict is its ability to bring to the surface what has been submerged. Conflict brings to light things that were not seen by one or both of you. Conflict helps to illuminate things that were in the shadows. Then you can address them and they can really go away, and not pretend-go-away. No more lumpy carpeting.

Here are some helpful hints about handling conflict:

Don't let little things that bother you build up until you explode. If it wasn't important enough to bring up within a couple days, then let it go.

If either of you doesn't want to talk about it right away, set a time to do so. It's another myth that you shouldn't go to bed angry; it's OK because you need your rest. You can agree on a time when you will meet. You can also agree at the start how long you will talk—because you need a breather, or because you have another commitment.

Don't ambush your spouse in order to put them at a disadvantage. It's unfair to catch them unawares, or to argue in public so you can "put them on the spot" in front of others by shaming them. If in public, postpone the disagreement until you have appropriate privacy.

Normally, it's not a good idea to fight in front of your kids if it's a long serious argument, heavy on the emotions. On the other hand, it can helpful for your children to see their parents disagree, if the parents can model healthy efforts to resolve their differences.

Finally, speed is not a practical goal. Talking faster or keeping the disagreement (and don't interrupt!) as short as possible is not proof that you did it well. Take time to think before you speak!

Practice dealing with conflict during your courtship and it will pay off in the long run.

PARTING THOUGHT

"The concept of two people living together for 25 years without a serious dispute suggests a lack of spirit only to be admired in sheep."[1]

FOR FURTHER REFLECTION

Think of two occasions at work—one when you dealt more successfully with conflict, and one when you didn't. How did your behavior contribute to resolution (or not)?

What is your personal fear of what will happen if you engage in conflict? Is there anything that helps you move past that fear?

How did your parents argue, and how did you feel when you saw it? What is it like when you are with other people who are fighting in public?

1. Herbert, *AZ Quotes.*

22

Love Always Leads to Change

MYTHICAL THINKING

The beautiful thing about love relationships is how they lead to change. For example, as soon as you let your partner know about something which irritates you, they will make the necessary change so that you are no longer bothered *because they love you*. Any time the two of you have a disagreement, whether it is about how to hang the roll of toilet paper or how to vote in the next presidential election, the disagreement will be almost immediately resolved because your partner will change his or her mind to agree with you *because they love you*.

Like every other normal person in the universe, your partner naturally gravitates to change. (Ignore Myth 15.) Your partner has no desire to have a personal opinion or a preferred way of doing things. Your partner *wants* to change, and is just waiting for the next opportunity to do so.

Therefore, if your relationship is built on true love, you have every right to expect that your partner will change. If your partner really loves you, they will change *for you*—happily, quickly, and with utter disregard for themselves, always. That is the beauty of love.

Some couples find that this dynamic does not "kick in" as quickly for them as it does for all other couples. It turns out that this is your fault! You have failed to love your spouse enough to be worthy of their willingness to change because of their love for you. However, if you love them hard enough, they will change. That's the power of your love—it is strong enough to make your partner want to change!

ON SECOND THOUGHT . . .

This myth is like Hydra, a multi-headed beast, which shows up with a variety of faces. Each face has some tattoo that proposes that one person has the power to make another person change—presto, change-o! Good luck with that. No one has that much power.

More likely each person in the relationship is inclined to settle into "comfort-mode," and making a change is almost always uncomfortable. A rule of science might serve as a rule of thumb for relationships: *For every action, there is an equal and opposite reaction.* So every time you push your spouse, it might help if you expect your spouse will react by pushing back, not by rolling over.

If you're not so sure about that scientific principle, try this simple experiment. Ask your spouse to tell you what *you* do that is irritating, and then see how you respond.

Here's a surprise for some couples—your spouse may have the same expectation for you as you do for your spouse—that *you* will naturally change as soon as a disagreement comes up—happily, quickly, and always!

When you express disagreement or say something that you'd like your partner to change, the assumption is that there's only one response—your partner makes the change. Actually, there are at least three possible responses: your partner changes, you change, or something else.

For example, for Thanksgiving dinner you want turkey and your partner wants ham. So your partner can change (and serves turkey), you can change (and eat ham), or you do something else (salmon will be the main course this year).

Love does not replace the hard work of change, although it may provide some motivation.

PARTING THOUGHT

"Love seems the swiftest, but it is the slowest of all growths. No man or woman really knows what perfect love is until they have been married a quarter of a century."[1]

FOR FURTHER REFLECTION

What are you waiting for your partner to change? How long have you been waiting?

How many things have you changed about yourself because your partner asked you to? How many things has your partner changed because you asked? Do you recognize all the things on your partner's list?

What motivates you to do something that will be difficult? How long does it take for you to decide, and then to actually do it?

1. Twain, *At Your Fingertips*, 248.

23

Remember That You Are Always Right; Remind Your Partner of This Frequently

MYTHICAL THINKING

This myth can help establish a strong foundation in your marriage. Whenever there's a disagreement, your spouse will already know that it's going to be resolved "your way," and this will save you both a lot of trouble that could otherwise be wasted in disagreements and negotiations.

Sometime early on in your relationship you may have had to explain *why* you are always right. There are several reasons to choose from or you may already have one of your own—

because you are the head of the house

because you are more educated

because you make more money

because your job is more important (esp. if you make less money)

because you are older (or, you have more life experience)

because you have been married more times than your spouse (so you have more experience)

because you are taller

because your family came over on the *Mayflower*.

At some point your spouse could forget what reason you provided. So it's helpful to remind your partner. Constant reminders are often overlooked as a helpful tool in your marital toolkit (see also Myth 13).

After you have laid the foundation, you don't have to give a cogent reason or provide any facts to support your decision or royal proclamations. Stick to the core truth—you are always right. Case closed.

ON SECOND THOUGHT . . .

Alas, some spouses will persist in a desire to discuss things when the two of you do not see eye to eye. Here are some helpful do's and don'ts:

1. Listen closely to what your spouse is saying. Listen so well that you understand, and could even convincingly make the same point to someone else on your spouse's behalf. Don't listen only with the intention of finding your next point of attack.

2. Describe your feelings, rather than letting them grow to the point that they can overwhelm you or your partner when they're expressed. Strong feelings can keep you wrapped up in yourself and unable to listen carefully to your partner. Try to look at your spouse when you're talking to one another. If the feelings are not too big, perhaps you can hold hands while you speak with each other.

3. If you find yourself getting louder, your partner will likely also get louder. Step back and take a breather so you can regain a sense of peace.

4. No hitting below the belt. Don't aim for your partner's vulnerabilities and pressure points. Causing pain does not make your point; it just leaves wounds and resentment.

5. Intimacy means you know their weaknesses and enduring vulnerabilities. So don't inflict pain to make your point.

6. Humor can sometimes help. Exercise caution, however, because teasing can be misinterpreted as minimizing your partner's thoughts and feelings, and causing hurt rather than bringing relief to the tension.

7. Respect and courtesy are essential rules (don't interrupt) for fighting fair in marriage.

An interesting technique is to engage in role-reversal: Have a discussion in which you switch places—you argue your partner's position and allow your spouse to present your position. Allow yourselves to see your spouse's point of view.

PARTING THOUGHT

"Confidence comes not from always being right but from not fearing to be wrong."[1]

FOR FURTHER REFLECTION

Do other people think that "you think you're always right?" What did you do or say that allowed them to reach this conclusion? Why do you suppose some people refuse to accept this fact?

Which of the seven constructive guidelines above does your partner do well? How do they affect your communication, especially in stressful situations?

Which of the seven guidelines above do you do well? How do they affect your communication, especially in stressful situations?

1. McIntyre, *AZ Quotes*.

24

Take Credit for Everything That Goes Well

MYTHICAL THINKING . . .

You are such a catch, your spouse is lucky to have you! You bring to your marriage an incredible combination of talents, skills, positive attributes and character traits, strong virtues, and an amazing set of accomplishments. You really have your act together. On top of all this, *la crème de la crème,* is your humility (though it's embarrassing when you have to point it out).

In your magnificent generosity, you have been willing to accept your partner, despite the fact of bringing into your relationship a whole lot of faults, mistakes, weaknesses, limitations, and wrong ways of doing things. Your spouse has at least a suitcase full of that stuff, if not a whole set of mismatched luggage.

Fortunately, along with your generosity, you are also filled with keen insight and patience. Your insight will allow you to notice with an eagle's eyes the contents of your partner's luggage, and be able to describe the contents with ease. Your virtue of patience will allow you to tolerate their existence (at least for a while). After all, you should not be expected to simply live with them forever. You deserve a *better* spouse than the one you married.

There is another gift that you can use to help your spouse. Your fantastic memory allows you to remember everything in their luggage, and to be able to articulate the list of contents on a moment's notice when you think your partner could use a good reminder. Your partner, in turn, will be eternally grateful for the extra attention you are giving to him or her by remembering all their faults, mistakes, weaknesses, limitations, and wrong ways of doing things.

ON SECOND THOUGHT . . .

How would you feel if this described the way your spouse thinks about you? Or maybe that's exactly what's already happening? Would it help your relationship to be thought of as *the problem?* Chances are pretty good that these same thoughts of yours don't help your partner either. Pointing a finger at someone usually accomplishes very little.

A healthy partnership will recognize that you both bring into the relationship your own luggage. You will also realize that you can accomplish much more by accepting responsibility for your own thoughts, emotions, and behavior than blaming your spouse for them. You can grow closer to your spouse by giving loving attention to your own list of faults, mistakes, weaknesses, limitations, and wrong ways of doing things. Your list might not be as obvious to you as your spouse's list, but it deserves as much dedicated effort as you expect from your spouse.

PARTING THOUGHT

"Whenever you're wrong, admit it; whenever you're right, shut up."[1]

---

1. Nash, "A Word to Husbands," 72.

FOR FURTHER REFLECTION

What are the contents of your luggage containing your faults, mistakes, weaknesses, limitations, and wrong ways of doing things? How many bags is that?

Do you enjoy being reminded about such things? How often is enough?

How can you help your spouse carry his or her luggage so you can enjoy your journey together?

25

Spouses Should Keep Score

MYTHICAL THINKING

Fair is fair, and if a marriage is nothing else, it should be fair.

This kind of arrangement can be called a CPA marriage (Conduct Precise Accounting), because it looks like two book-keepers working very hard to keep their spreadsheets balanced:

"If I did something extra for her, I now expect that she will do something extra for me (and it should be something that I choose)."

"If he neglected something he was supposed to do, then I get to neglect one of my responsibilities."

"If she spent fifty dollars on my birthday present, then I don't have to spend more than fifty dollars on hers (plus or minus a dollar)."

"I'll be happy to do what you asked, but what will you do for me?"

This appears to be the application of a scientific principle: For every action there is an equal and opposite reaction. The belief is that both of you must give careful attention to what each of you has done or not done, so it can be matched by the other. A positive action must be matched by a positive action; and an act of negligence or negativity also gets to be matched by a similar act.

Tit for tat; *quid pro quo*; fair is fair.

ON SECOND THOUGHT . . .

The dilemma is not that you are engaging in acts of kindness and generosity. Equal is not necessarily equitable. The problem is an assumption that your actions must be counted and tracked like plusses and minuses on a marriage-calculator. This *quid pro quo* occurs in unhappy marriages when each of you feels the need to keep a running tally of who has done (or not done) what for whom.

When you are reasonably happy, you'll do nice things simply because you feel good about your spouse and your relationship. Acts of kindness and generosity will occur naturally, and they don't have to be tracked in a marriage app on your phone. You will find satisfaction and joy in doing things that please and surprise your partner. You'll be alert for opportunities to help ease a burden or to extend a helping hand. You'll be glad that you are also on the receiving end of your partner's kindness and generosity.

These acts don't have to be huge. Bringing your spouse a glass of water, performing an errand that the other partner prefers not to do, being present for an activity that's important to your spouse—these show that you care, and they have the added benefit of re-filling your partner's reservoir of good will.

Equal is not necessarily equitable. Instead of making sure everything is balanced 50–50, here's another attitude to try: Even though you're already contributing more than 50% to your marital relationship, you still want to do more.

PARTING THOUGHT

"A good marriage is a contest of generosity."[1]

1. Sawyer, *AZ Quotes*.

FOR FURTHER REFLECTION

What does it mean to be fair to your partner? Can it be measured?

In your marriage, do you keep track of who has done what? Do you engage in paybacks when you've been hurt or neglected?

Which of you contributes more to your relationship? If your partner is the generous one, can you do more? Even if you're the generous one, can you do more?

26

Always Blame Your Partner for Your Problems

MYTHICAL THINKING

Let's not beat around the bush here. If there's a problem in your relationship, then it's got to be someone's fault. So it's not only efficient but probably true that your spouse is to blame for whatever's gone wrong.

To maintain support for this stance, it's important that you stay on the offense by being incredibly helpful to your partner—demonstrate your generosity, your keen insight, your patience, and your memory. Otherwise there might be the teensy tiny thought in the back of your mind that there is a teensy tiny possibility that you may be partially responsible for some small portion of the difficulties in your relationship. You must obliterate this thought as soon as possible before it has any chance to take root in your consciousness.

You can strengthen your blaming techniques in several ways:

1. Do whatever is necessary to keep the focus of attention where it belongs—on your partner who's to blame. Do not allow

your spouse to point a finger at you for anything, because that's a slippery slope that sooner or later will take you down to the pit of blame.

2. Point out to your partner that your life would be so much better if it weren't for the "baggage" that your spouse brings to this relationship. You would be more successful, more affectionate, more helpful, *more* _____ *(fill in the blank)* if not for your spouse. You would also be a better spouse, a better parent, a better lover, *a better* _____ *(fill in the blank)*, if only your spouse would follow your helpful suggestions and constant reminders.

3. Resist all efforts to allow anyone to turn the spotlight on you or your attitudes or your behaviors. This will get you nowhere. Help other people to see where the real problem lies—with your spouse. Even if you did something, point out that your partner made you do it.

4. You must also hold your spouse responsible for your feelings. In no case are you accountable for your own emotions; you are merely the victim of your partner's words and actions which make you feel the way you do. Therefore, you must control your spouse because that is the person who controls how you feel. You have to manage your spouse so that you can be happy, and not allow your spouse to make you feel sad or bad or angry.

5. Also resist efforts to accept responsibility together as a couple. People may say things like "we both got caught up in this." This can be a sneaky effort to include you as part of the problem, and it must be squashed like a bug.

6. There also may be efforts to say there is no room for the "blame game," and that both of you should move on. They might assert that "it's no one's fault," or "it just happened." Point out that they are in denial and refusing to see where the problem really is—in your partner.

7. Finally having clearly established who is to blame, you must also claim the right and responsibility to punish your partner in any way that you see fit. Anyone in their right mind will be able to see that it is clearly deserved.

ON SECOND THOUGHT . . .

Even if one spouse has a difficulty of some kind, the other spouse's response can make it ten times worse.

The guidelines above have the potential to do all that, and more.

The task in a heathy relationship is to identify both your own responsibility as well as your partner's responsibility in each situation. It takes two to tango. Hardly ever is it all the fault of one person.

PARTING THOUGHT

"All married couples should learn the art of battle as they should learn the art of making love. Good battle is objective and honest— never vicious or cruel. Good battle is healthy and constructive, and brings to a marriage the principles of equal partnership."[1]

FOR FURTHER REFLECTION

Has your partner adopted any of the seven "guidelines" above? How does that affect your relationship?

Do you follow any of the seven "guidelines" above? How does that affect your relationship?

Are there any behaviors you could adopt to replace any of the problematic behaviors described above?

Can you write a new set of guidelines that helps you take responsibility for your part in a difficult situation?

1. Landers, *AZ Quotes.*

27

Your Spouse Is Always the Cause of Financial Problems in Your Marriage

MYTHICAL THINKING

Money is great! More money is better. Maybe even better than sex if you have enough.

More money automatically gives you the security and stability of not having to worry about whether you have enough money. You don't have to worry if your clothes are out of fashion because you can shop whenever you like (unless there's a pandemic). You have enough money not to worry about whether you can feed yourself and your family because you can buy all the groceries you need, and eat out as often as you like. You don't have to worry about whether you have a safe place to live because you can buy locks and fences and alarm systems and security guards. You don't have to worry about your car breaking down because you can always buy a new one. More money means total security.

More money also means freedom to do whatever you want. You can travel wherever you want, have as big a house as you want, plus a vacation home that's also as big as you want. You can buy any new thing you see in a catalog that catches your fancy. You can click on an ad while you're online and have it delivered to your house the next day. It doesn't matter how much you have because you can always rent more storage space. Having more money means you can do whatever you want.

So make sure the majority of your time in your marriage is devoted to making money so that you can buy all the security and freedom you deserve. More money will bring your marriage to the pinnacle of success and happiness while making you the envy of other married couples who don't have as much money.

A fly in the ointment may be your spouse, who doesn't want to spend money like you do—who wants to spend (or save), who wants to donate to different places than you do, who handles a checkbook differently than you do. It's obvious that your spouse is the one person who stands in your way of having enough money for perfect fun and freedom. In sooooo many ways your spouse is the source of a major problem in your marriage. Your partner doesn't really understand finances with the same sharp expertise that you have, and is doing the financial stuff all wrong.

ON SECOND THOUGHT . . .

Money is just like sex—they are both important in your marriage and they don't magically take care of themselves. More marriages may break up because of finances than any other reason.

More money can help with stability, security, and freedom in your relationship. It can also foster selfishness, cause stress, and lead to arguments. Think about whether a lack of agreement about your finances adds stress and anxiety to your lives.

Financial management is significant because it concretely expresses your beliefs and values in your everyday life. Having discussions about your financial resources does not always mean that you lack money. It may be that you don't agree on how you're going to spend it. Some common questions that couples grapple with include:

What do you choose to buy and not buy?

How much do you save, and for what?

Do you have a budget, and stick by it?

Do you have separate checking accounts or share one, and why?

What do you invest in, and what is your rationale for those choices?

Do you plan for the future or live in the moment?

Do you make donations, and for what causes?

How do you handle debt?

What plans have you made for financial emergencies?

How much will you need for retirement, and how will you get that?

What will you do with a windfall like an inheritance, a tax refund, or a stimulus check?

What are the responsibilities for each of you in caring for your finances—paying bills, choosing investments, preparing a budget, tracking your expenses?

Financial management is also important because it's an expression of the health or dysfunction of your relationship. Do you trust your spouse making decisions about your finances? Does one of you hide purchases or credit cards or savings from the other?

Couples in healthy marriages are much more likely to have significant conversations about money. Yet many couples report that money is the issue they argued about the most, and therefore want to avoid those discussions. Difficulties with finances is one of the more common issues in marriage; you are not alone.[1]

Money is an important issue in marriage, and everything that doesn't go well is not your spouse's fault. But finances don't take care of themselves; they require attention and planning.

There are good resources available to help you. The best sources of information and reasonable expectations about finances

1. Ramsey Solutions.

are not found on the backs of cereal boxes or advertisements for another credit card. Look for some reputable sources or a Certified Financial Planner to obtain the expert assistance you both deserve.

PARTING THOUGHT

"I came to realize that my money problems, worries, and shortages largely began and ended with the person in the mirror."[2]

FOR FURTHER REFLECTION

What are your goals or how much income do you require for a satisfying lifestyle? How did you determine this amount? Does your partner agree?

How long do you expect it will take to achieve your financial goals? What are the steps you will take to reach those goals?

What are some ordinary or extraordinary things that could interfere with achieving those goals?

2. Ramsey, *The Total Money Makeover*, 3.

28

Engage in "Marital Archeology" by Digging up the Past

MYTHICAL THINKING

One of the ways that you can be helpful to your spouse is to encourage the recollection and disclosure of painful memories. Then you can add to your partner's regret for having shared that personal information with you by misusing it and making them feel worse.

You can also be helpful by accepting their tidbits and then digging around for more information. Don't presume that you have been told everything or that it was accurate. It is much more likely that there are other "nuggets of gold" still hidden. You should diligently strive to uncover them (even if your spouse does not want you to).

Keep these painful revelations in the forefront of your spouse's mind. Do not let your partner forget them, thereby losing any advantages gained through constant references to their suffering.

Your knowledge of your partner's past will help you help your partner. You can point out to your partner that the contents of the old trunks in the attic are connected to the luggage that is possessed now. You can help your partner realize how their past is contributing to the marital struggles which exist now, and the past is to blame (see Myth 26).

Give helpful reminders like, "You remind me so much of your mother" (and make sure that it's not misunderstood as a compliment, which misses the whole point!). Say things like, "Your old girlfriend told me that you would try that on me, too, and she was right!" If you can, use psychological language, which shows how well you understand your spouse, "You're a narcissist just like your dear ol' dad!" or "Is your whole family a bunch of drunks?"

ON SECOND THOUGHT . . .

People in a dispute will find it more helpful to look at the *problem* rather than pointing at the *person*. Most often the problem exists in the relationship between people rather than solely in one of the spouses. Looking at the topic of controversy rather than blaming your partner is more likely to produce a positive outcome.

Stick to the issue at hand; avoid bringing several problems into the same argument. It is not helpful to mention "everything plus the kitchen sink" which is overwhelming and makes resolution much more difficult. There's also a huge risk for hurt feelings, which leads to resentment rather than resolution.

Consider the difference between two ways to discuss a difficult and emotional issue. One way is to (literally or figuratively) sit across a table from one another, point fingers of blame, and say that your *spouse* is the problem. Another way is to (literally or figuratively) sit side by side at a table and examine the *problem* that is on the table in front of you. They are very different dynamics and can lead to very different results.

Trust each person's mind to reveal what it feels safe to reveal. Great damage can be done by digging around where you're not wanted and when a person is not ready. You don't have a right to dig around in someone else's painful history, not even your spouse's.

PARTING THOUGHT

"Archaeology is not a science; it's a vendetta."[1]

FOR FURTHER REFLECTION

What are some things that you prefer to keep private and not share with your spouse? What do you think will happen if those things come out into the light of day?

How do you feel when someone pushes in where they are not welcome? How do you respond?

Does your spouse say that you or your behavior is just like "So and so?" Is there a time when you and your partner had a discussion about a similar kind of accusation? What can you learn from the success or failure of that discussion?

1. Wheeler, from Hopkirk, *Foreign Devils*, 170.

29

Exaggerate the Negative and Minimize the Positive to Help Your Spouse Grow

MYTHICAL THINKING

First, think big. In order to help your spouse grow, it is important that you provide the fair and objective perspective of an outsider. You are in the best position as someone who knows them well to be able to point out their limitations, their weakness, their mistakes great and small, and most especially their failures. Let them know how disappointing they are to you by not living up to your expectations.

This is a great service to them so that they do not ever forget these things. You provide them the support they need by giving them regular reminders of their flawed behavior. This will motivate them to want to make a change and become a better partner for you.

The repetition will also help them to hear you better in case they missed the point during earlier listings of their offenses. It also helps them not simply that you state the facts, but for you to distort and exaggerate them to make their faults and failures clear.

It also makes it more difficult to disagree with you because, when they claim your facts are not true, you can accuse them of being defensive or blind to their own faults.

Second, you must balance your exaggeration with minimalization. Don't spend too much time pointing out your spouse's skills and good behavior. That will interfere with them building up a healthy self-esteem. Think small. Focus on undervaluing their accomplishments—"You weren't the only one who got a promotion." Trivialize what is positive, like "Losing fifty pounds is no big deal." And diminish anything that could lead to them "getting a big head"—you certainly don't want to live with anyone who has a big head!

When they have this new perspective that recognizes how puny they are, and how much they need to grow, it will enhance your status in their eyes—how fortunate they are to have you in their life! This will remind them how great you are to stay in a relationship with them despite their many shortcomings.

Finally, develop the skill of criticism. Move beyond specifics to broad sweeping statements. Move beyond particular behaviors to attacking their personality and character flaws. Let them see the big picture and not sweat the details.

ON SECOND THOUGHT . . .

Criticism is not a skill—it is a harmful behavior and destructive in a relationship. Its generality makes it hard for your spouse to neutralize.

Exaggeration is not helpful either. It doesn't "make your point" but instead distorts the truth into a misshapen caricature of a person you love.

Repetition is irritating. Let's be clear about this—repetition is irritating. Saying the same thing again and again makes it more likely that your partner will "turn you off" than hear you, because repetition is really irritating.

Negative Repetition, Exaggeration, and Criticism will REC (wreck) your marriage. It is hurtful, and when it comes from a spouse who is in the position to nurture, it makes things worse. There is nothing about REC-ing your partner that makes it a preferred approach.

Research tell us just the opposite—we need to hear the positive. We need to hear more affirmation so as not to be overwhelmed by any negative statements.

Couples who grow are those who listen and understand one another. They are partners who honor and respect each other. They are spouses who strengthen and build up, not tear down.

The rule is true: Think Big (lots of expressions of affection, support, and encouragement), and Think Small (keep the negativity to a minimum, because even a little lasts a long time).

PARTING THOUGHT

"Dishonest people conceal their faults from themselves as well as others; honest people know and confess them."[1]

FOR FURTHER REFLECTION

Can you name all the ways that your behavior is a disappointment to your spouse? Do you justify why those things are minor or unimportant and don't need to be changed?

Are there ways that each of you trivialize what the other partner has accomplished? How does it feel?

What are the ways that you support, encourage, and applaud your spouse? How often do you do them?

1. Bovee, *AZ Quotes.*

30

Give Your Partner an Abundance of Cold Pricklies; Warm Fuzzies Are Over-Rated

MYTHICAL THINKING

What are we talking about? "Cold Pricklies" refer to negative comments, criticisms, cutdowns, so-called "helpful suggestions," distancing remarks, undercutting, and name-calling. They refer to words that are bitter, mean-spirited, harsh, hurtful, and shaming.

Warm Fuzzies refer to compliments, supportive comments, affirmations, praise, accolades, commendations, approval, congratulations, sincere flattery, and verbal applause. They refer to words that promote intimacy, affection, and caring in a relationship.

You'll learn very soon that it's much more effective to direct a flurry of Cold Pricklies at your spouse. These will help your partner to know what you like and don't like. Then they will be in a better position to conform themselves to your preferences and maintain your happiness, which ought to be their #1 priority.

An abundance of Cold Pricklies helps your spouse know what is unsuitable in their character and their behavior so that they can improve. Don't worry about hurting your partner's feelings—your partner should already know you love them. So you don't have to hold back from stating the obvious, and your spouse will be grateful.

The fact is that Warm Fuzzies are vastly over-rated. They just coddle your spouse, and your indulging them with terms of endearment will turn them into complacent lumps of dough. Who wants to be married to a lump of dough?

ON SECOND THOUGHT . . .

Not many people are inclined to change when they have been attacked and their feelings have been hurt. Your plan to give your partner lots of Cold Pricklies is not likely to get you very far, and may actually set you back. You may know the saying: You can catch more flies with honey than vinegar. (This is good to know if you like to catch flies!) More importantly, truthful sweet-talk is more likely to be accepted by your spouse and to affirm your affection than expressing bitterness and displeasure.

Some people get confused, however, and instead they give *Warm* Pricklies and *Cold* Fuzzies. Such comments are like skunks—looking all soft and cuddly, but inside they are loaded for attack. Another image is "a steel fist in a velvet glove"—what is the person shaking your hand really trying to express—friendship or aggression?

It's like telling a bull in a china shop to be gentle—it's baffling, and therefore not effective communication. Then you can't understand why your partner is not responding as you had hoped. These are sometimes called "mixed messages" or "backhanded compliments." For example, when you say, "Those pants really hide how fat you are!" your spouse is left wondering how to respond—was it a compliment about the pants or a hurtful comment about being overweight?

Try using more honey and less vinegar.

PARTING THOUGHT

"Seeing you lights up my day, to hear your voice makes me smile all cheesy, to see you smile makes my heart all warm and fuzzy, when you say 'I love you' makes my body weak."[1]

FOR FURTHER REFLECTION

If your spouse gives you Cold Pricklies, how do you respond?

How do you feel when you receive Warm Fuzzies? What happens as a result?

Have you ever been accused of sending confusing or mixed messages? How does this interfere with your communications with your spouse? What steps could you take personally to improve your communication?

1. Gardner, *AZ Quotes.*

31

Never Ever Forgive Your Spouse

MYTHICAL THINKING

When your spouse has treated you unfairly or harmed you in some way, it is important that you do not forgive them. No matter how many times they ask, how much that you are begged, no matter the promises made or the changes that you see, no matter how much repentance or remorse is shown, do not give in and grant forgiveness.

Your forgiveness will be a sign of weakness that they can use against you again and again. Your forgiveness undercuts the position of superiority you now hold over your spouse, and to forgive would be like the strong man Samson cutting off his own hair.

Always hold your partner's wrongdoing in your back pocket, so you can pull it out when needed and remind your spouse how you were hurt. It's better to hang on to your pain and to keep it fresh, and always to remember how you were wronged, betrayed, and treated unfairly by someone who supposedly loves you. This behavior is the lifeblood for your "inner martyr," while you publicly demonstrate to your family your goodness and long-suffering patience. Keep your pain alive because it will energize you even though it is killing you.

ON SECOND THOUGHT . . .

It is not surprising that many people who have been hurt in some way have a strong reaction to the idea of forgiveness. When you have been wounded, you can usually give several reasons why you won't consider the option of forgiveness. Your reasons can sound very reasonable.

Your resistance may be rooted in a misunderstanding about the nature of forgiveness itself. You may think that forgiveness is something that's "given" to the offender, which seems unjust if not absolutely ridiculous—why should the one who was victimized give anything to the perpetrator?

It is important to remember, then, that forgiveness is a process to help the injured person, not the one who caused the harm. To refuse to engage in the process of forgiveness is like saying, "I refuse to heal." It's like eating poisonous mushrooms and then waiting for someone else to die.

Forgiveness is a process of healing that decreases your pain and suffering; it relieves you of heavy burdens you are carrying around. When you have suffered deeply, you have thoughts, feelings, and behaviors that are directly related to your injuries. Those wounds persist, causing more pain; they do not simply disappear with the passage of time. Forgiveness is the process in which you change your thoughts, feelings, and behaviors in order to heal and live a healthier and more satisfying life.

Research shows that forgiveness helps restore your sense of personal power and freedom. It moves you toward more positive emotions, and increases both your physical and mental health. It also improves the quality of your interpersonal relationships.

While you might prefer that the healing process of forgiveness proceed smoothly and gradually, it actually has lots of ups and downs, forward movement and reversals. It's helpful to keep that in mind so that you don't think you've done it wrong or failed.

If there is no forgiveness in your marriage, you'll be left carrying around a garbage bag of wrongdoings. This will make it nearly impossible to enjoy your relationship.

PARTING THOUGHT

"You cannot forgive too much. The weak can never forgive. Forgiveness is the attribute of the strong."[1]

FOR FURTHER REFLECTION

Do you find yourself holding grudges? What does it feel like? What could it feel like if you were no longer holding them?

Is there someone significant in your life who has refused to forgive you? How does that affect your relationship?

What reasons do you say to yourself about why you won't forgive?

1. Ghandi, "Interview to the Press."

32

The Only Way to Express Affection in Marriage Is to Have Sex

MYTHICAL THINKING

Sex is great! Maybe the best thing in the whole world (besides sharing warm chocolate chip cookies and milk with your partner).

Sex is not only great, it's important because it's the only way you can show your partner your deep feelings of affection. That's why it's called "making love."

So when you really love your spouse, the result will be that every time you make love you will have simultaneous orgasms (which are definitely way better than sharing warm chocolate cookies and milk with your partner). These will be mind-blowing, earth-shattering, bed-breaking orgasms. They can occur several times a day, but at least once a day is the national norm.

This is what will make your marriage a blissful success, because the result of your daily orgasmic ecstasy leads to marital nirvana. Your sex life will make your relationship heaven on earth.

Therefore, you know by now that it's important that you be the best lover in the whole world.

Fortunately, this magnificent vision is easily attainable for every couple because it all happens quite naturally. This is not some "pie in the sky ideal" accessible only to a select few. Unlike athletes who must be coached and train their bodies to achieve greatness, "sex" takes care of itself because it's natural and biological.

This is the promise of marriage. If it's not happening for you, then your marriage is a shipwreck. There's obviously something wrong with you (actually, more likely there's something majorly wrong with your partner) (see Myths 24, 26, and 34). Please, do not let anyone know about this tragedy which is easily fixed. Don't worry, because you'll be up and making ecstatic orgasmic love in no time.

In order to deal with this devastating marital misfortune, you must have more sex and achieve more simultaneous orgasms. Fortunately, with little or no effort, this will happen and you will save your marriage. But in case it doesn't happen right away, persevere and do not lose hope. You just need to have more sex in order to achieve the orgasmic nirvana that all your friends and neighbors are enjoying. Then you can hold your head high because you have what everyone else has.

ON SECOND THOUGHT . . .

OK, let's get real now. Sorry to pop your balloons, but you and your partner actually will be relieved in the long run when your sex life does not match the description you just read. You would be exhausted, your significant body parts would collapse from overuse, and there would be no time to take care of the kids who come as a result (because no means of contraception is foolproof).

Yes, sex is great and it's an important part of married life. It is a profound way to express and receive love between spouses. But it's not the only way, and you could unfairly over-emphasize sex in a way that actually harms your relationship.

There are many ways to express your love for your partner, including spending time and enjoying activities together, facial expressions, physical touch, words of affirmation and affection, self-disclosure, acts of service, and self-sacrifice. Likewise, a sexual relationship is not limited to sexual intercourse. Other ways to demonstrate sexual affection include touch and massage, kissing, foreplay, and oral sexual activity.

Be careful about the "Facebook phenomenon"—that everyone is enjoying blissful lives as seen on their Facebook pages. It's simply not true that everyone is having sex several times a day—except you. Maybe you've heard this truism: put a penny into a jar each time you make love during your first year of marriage. Then take a penny out each time you make love starting the second year. There will still be pennies in your jar when you die.

Please note that the success of your marriage is not dependent on your perfect lovemaking. Even multi-orgasmic sexual intercourse won't sustain a marriage or turn an unhappy marriage into an ecstatic one. It's interesting to note that a significant percentage of people have regular consensual sexual relations with their former spouses after the divorce; which underlines the premise that while the sex is fine, it was not enough to keep them married.

The sexual dimension is significant in marriage. But it's not automatic and doesn't "take care of itself." It requires attention and practice just like other significant dimensions, such as communication, finances, conflict resolution, and raising children. Difficulty in a sexual relationship is one of the more common issues in marriage; you are not alone.

Lovemaking is also affected by the everyday reality of life, not something turned on and off like an electrical switch. How did the day go? Are the children longing for attention? Are you still angry with one another? Were you nearly injured in a car accident? Did your boss call you out for a stupid mistake? How you feel, how you are thinking about yourself, and how you are thinking and feeling about your partner all have a massive impact on your sexual activity.

There are good resources available to help you. The best sources of information and reasonable expectations about sexual relations are not romance novels from the grocery store and pornographic videos which you can watch day or night with a couple of clicks. Look for some reputable sources or a trained counselor to receive the assistance you both deserve.

PARTING THOUGHT

"The chief cause of unhappiness in married life is that people think that marriage is sex attraction."[1]

FOR FURTHER REFLECTION

What are ways that you can express affection to your spouse besides sex? Does your spouse have some ways that are preferred? Do you have some ways besides sex that you would like your partner to express affection to you? Have you shared this information with one another?

What are parts of your ordinary life that interfere with your sexual relationship? Does your partner answer the same way or are there other things?

Is there anything more you would like to learn about love-making? Are you willing?

---

1. Tolstoy, AZ Quotes.

33

Hitting Is Permissible and Necessary in Marriage

MYTHICAL THINKING

It's OK to twist and pull her hair because she talked back to you. It's fine to hit him with a pan because he needs to be punished. It's fine to push your partner against a wall and threaten maiming because you need to teach them a lesson with a little physical reinforcement. Sexual violence against your partner is allowed because you're married.

The crimes of assault, battery, harassment, and rape between strangers and acquaintances are perfectly acceptable when spouses do the same thing.

ON SECOND THOUGHT . . .

This myth is a "double-header" because both the do-er and the receiver may believe it.

The one who commits abuse of any sort tries to justify the behavior. Likewise the one who is the victim of abuse may also try to justify the behavior with a belief that for some reason they earned it or deserve it (and so it's not really abuse).

We're very serious here, so listen up! Both attempts at justification are just plain nonsense. This is not behavior that belongs in marriage. It is one person exercising power and control over the other one, plain and simple.

No matter what excuse exists in your mind, and no matter what reason your partner gives—threats, harm, or violence—none of it is acceptable. Period. End of story.

Do not tolerate any such behavior directed toward you. If your partner breaks the promise to never do that again—even once—then you have already given them a second chance, and they blew it.

Do not hurt the one you love. Spouses should be like doctors who make an oath: Do no harm.

Be very careful about other forms of violence as well. Don't use your words as weapons—harsh words, name-calling, labelling, and "psychologizing" your partner are not likely to get you closer to resolution of challenges in your relationship. Do no harm.

If by chance something does slip out of your mouth in the heat of the moment, exercise the 5-second rule. Acknowledge it immediately and apologize for what you said; ask your partner to let you "take it back" so it doesn't distract from the true issue at hand.

Be careful about the tone of your voice. There is a big difference between a conversation and yelling at one another. Avoid sarcasm, which totally contradicts the nice words you may be saying. Do no harm.

Finally, avoid anything that can appear intimidating, such as standing over your spouse who is seated, or approaching your partner in a hurried manner. Even your touch can be misinterpreted if the other partner is not ready. You may think you're giving consolation, but at that moment your spouse may feel unsafe or violated because you stepped within their boundaries of safety.

PARTING THOUGHT

"Chains do not hold a marriage together. It is threads, hundreds of tiny threads, which sew people together through the years."[1]

FOR FURTHER REFLECTION

What is it like for you when you witness an act of physical violence? What is the impact on the victim?

Are there any occasions when you believe that physical, emotional, or verbal abuse is acceptable? What does your partner say about that?

What damage to the relationship do you think might occur when physical or psychological abuse takes place between spouses? How do you imagine it affects the children who see it?

1. Signoret, "Talking to David Lewin," 7.

Your Dream Marriage

Paradise Lost

Sad to say, sometimes good will and good intentions are not enough. Sometimes one or more of the myths gets a grip on you, and you make a good effort to make that myth come true. Alas, it is a myth; and your efforts fail to deliver the bliss you hoped for.

Truth be told, there are "seasons" in relationships and marriages. Your successful partnership will not be a series of calibrated steps in a steady climb to the mountaintop of blessed perfection. Marriages change over time; stability is not an enduring state of marriage.

Couples in a healthy marriage will have the skills and flexibility to adapt. They will show resilience as they adjust to the changes that come with the changes in a common marital life cycle that can include in-laws; children being born, growing up, and leaving; aging, and aging parents; working and retirement. Couples may also have to deal with unpredictable events like natural disasters, sudden unemployment, physical accidents, and illnesses.

It is unlikely that your entire marriage will go "according to plan." There will be days of joy and days of pain, some of them because of the person to whom you committed yourself, and some that you caused all by yourself. However, something not going right doesn't mean it's a catastrophe.

Every couple, and every spouse, has a reservoir of good will. They can tolerate for a while, look the other way, and make excuses.

Over time, however, the reservoir can be drained by the pricks of sharp words, the repetition of wrongs, or calamitous events from within or from outside the marriage.

What do you do then?

PARTING THOUGHT

"Almost no one is foolish enough to imagine that he automatically deserves great success in any field of activity; yet almost everyone believes that he automatically deserves success in marriage."[1]

1. Harris, *AZ Quotes.*

34

If Your Marriage Is Not Going Well, Then It's Obviously Your Fault, Which Means You're Unlovable and Worthless

MYTHICAL THINKING

Most spouses know right away that, if something is not going well in a marriage, their spouse is to blame. It's common sense (see Myth 26).

However, there is a special group of people who know the real truth—that if something goes wrong, it has absolutely nothing to do with their spouse. They have a switch in their brain whose default position is set at self-blame. If anything goes wrong, the automatic conclusion is "It's my fault." (You know if this is you.)

So if you were a *good* partner, you would be able to provide everything necessary to make your marriage successful and happy (see Myths 1–5). But that's not the case in your marriage, and you know who's to blame for that, because you are fundamentally flawed. At your core you are a miserable excuse for a human being, and you don't know what your partner saw in you in the first place.

You should never have married (anyone) because of this basic flaw in your makeup. From the start your relationship was doomed to fail because of the deficiencies at the core of your being.

You not only *feel* unloved and worthless, you know that you are unlovable and have no value whatsoever. You're using up the natural resources of this planet and have nothing to contribute. Your marriage never had a chance because you were involved.

ON SECOND THOUGHT . . .

Excuse the French, but this is a crock! It's a multi-car pileup of untruths, false assumptions, and illogical conclusions.

If you were a teacher, would you allow your students to write such things about themselves? If you were a parent, would you allow your children to believe such things about themselves? Then why is it OK to talk about yourself in such a demeaning manner? *Really???*

It's time to get off the pity pot and face the truth.

You are a human being, no less deserving of respect, affection, and healthy intimate relationships than any other person on this planet. You are a unique combination of strengths and flaws, virtues and vices, with your own personal history of successes and failures, mistakes and accomplishments. None of that rules out marriage for you or anyone else.

As for your marriage—it takes two to make that relationship, so you can't hog all the credit if it's not going well.

Nevertheless, some words of caution are appropriate. This kind of trashy self-talk may affect your behavior (inside or outside your marriage). An acquaintance often struggles with confidence and self-blame. You can say to her, "Wow, you look great in that red dress," and she will say, "I know, I know, I should have worn the blue one." You may be gathering and storing a harvest of negative experiences to validate your negative perception of yourself.

When there's a hint that something might not go well, or might not go your way, then you may try to protect yourself by going on the offense. You may believe it's better to be unfriendly before someone is unfriendly to you; to attack before someone attacks you (verbally or physically); to hurt before you get hurt.

Sometimes you may even do things unconsciously that prompt other people to treat you badly. If you start a sentence by saying "This is a really stupid idea . . . ," who's going to listen to what you say?

So while you can't hog all the credit, you can take responsibility for the part you play.

PARTING THOUGHT

"The power that connection holds in our lives was confirmed when the main concern about connection emerged as the fear of disconnection; the fear that something we have done or failed to do, something about who we are or where we come from, has made us unlovable and unworthy of connection."[1]

FOR FURTHER REFLECTION

How do you talk to yourself about yourself? While on some level you believe what you are saying is true, would your closest friend agree with your assessment?

Do you naturally tend to take the blame for anything that goes wrong? Is that fair to yourself? Could anyone else share responsibility for what is happening in your life?

Do you believe what goes well or not so well in a marriage is due to both people, or do you think it's just due to one of the partners? Can you think of some examples to support your thinking?

1. Brown, *AZ Quotes.*

35

When Your Marriage Is Strained, Seek Advice from Everyone Who Will Listen to You

MYTHICAL THINKING

Usually when there are difficulties in a marriage, the spouses themselves without any training will be able to diagnose and treat the issue. You will know precisely what is needed and how to provide it, and work very hard to fix your spouse. But just in case that's not true for you, the good news is that there are other people (single and divorced as well as married) who can step forward to offer assistance. Everyone will have ideas about how to fix your marriage. Let's look at some common sources to seek help.

Your Extended Family

Make sure that you share all your marital disagreements and troubles with all the members of your extended family. Include everyone so that no one feels left out. Facebook is handy to keep people informed about your troubles throughout the year. Family reunions and large holiday gatherings are also good times to tell everyone personally so they can weigh in and debate the problems and solutions; this also contributes to the festivity of the event.

Other People Who Are in Any Way Acquainted with Either of You

This group of people can provide you a significant amount of input because it is so encompassing. It can include your neighbors, your beautician, the mail carrier, the grocery checkout and the young person who takes your groceries out to the car; colleagues at work and the security guard who checks you in each day; people at church because they are never judgmental; and your friend who has been divorced three times and therefore really understands marriage. They all have an opinion. Because this group can be so large, you might find it's better to be selective and tell people who only know *you* because they are more likely to take your side.

ON SECOND THOUGHT . . .

There are better and worse ways to seek help. You don't need to drag your family into the intimacy of your marriage. Don't assume they will have objective insights because they know you so well. Don't approach them with the hope that they will give you more examples to prove you are right. Your parents and your in-laws are not disinterested bystanders; they are lions and lionesses who want to protect their children from harm by an "outsider."

Your children are no better equipped to be marital therapists than spouses are for themselves. Don't expect your children to be arbitrators in their parents' disputes. Don't push your children to choose sides; it puts them in a terrible position. It's like asking them to choose between cyanide and rat poison, when in fact the loss of either parent is likely to be traumatic.

It is also a breach of marital privacy to share your troubles with everyone and their brother and sister. Just because people have been married does not make them experts about marriage, any more than people who eat food are experts in nutrition or cooking. So well-meaning advice that helped a friend's marriage may not serve you well.

Seeking help from a trained marital therapist is a good option as long as you understand what a counselor will and will not do. They know that "not one size fits all," and what is helpful for one person or one couple may not help others.

Seeking professional help *is* a great option. However, many couples approach therapists as if they are oracles, magicians, or dictators. You may have a mistaken notion that the counselor will know exactly how to fix *your spouse's problems.* Don't expect to sit back and enjoy the therapy sessions while the counselor patiently explains to your spouse what they are doing wrong and how to do it right.

And please, don't remind your spouse that you are paying a counselor a boatload of money to tell your spouse the exact same things which you yourself had already pointed out. When you engage in marriage counseling, you are making an investment that may provide benefits for the rest of your life.

The aim of getting marital assistance is to heal your relationship, not to "fix your spouse." When you are in marital counseling, the client is the Relationship. The Relationship belongs to both partners. They both contribute to it and both have a vested interest in restoring it (even if it appears that one person has *the problem*). And so normally both partners participate in the therapy sessions.

You go to a surgeon to do something important that you can't do yourself. There's no shame in getting help to mend some marital wounds. As partners you are the ones who started the relationship and in the end you're the only ones who can heal it.

PARTING THOUGHT

"I have been doing marriage counseling for about 15 years and I realized that what makes one person feel loved, doesn't make another person feel loved."[1]

FOR FURTHER REFLECTION

Whom do you decide to tell about problems in your marriage? How did you decide on those people? Are those people trustworthy? Can they be objective, and do they have significant skills and experience to assist you?

Are you speaking about difficulties in your marriage as a way to win the battle with your spouse? Are you choosing people that you expect to take your side?

What sorts of questions would you ask a counselor when selecting someone to help you and your spouse resolve difficult issues? What would rule out a counselor for you?

1. Chapman, *AZ Quotes.*

36

Always Stay in a Dysfunctional Marriage So That Your Children Will Be OK

MYTHICAL THINKING

Children are very resilient creatures. They can withstand any number of difficulties and bounce right back again. You can probably name some famous person who had a hard childhood, surpassed their adversity, and is now successful. Facing hardship made them stronger, just like exercising and building up muscles.

So it makes sense to conclude that your toxic marital relationship will have no impact on your children either.

Children have a natural ability to deal with grownup stuff—like loud arguments; intoxicated behavior and seeing their parents "high"; exposure to violence (like throwing things, punching holes in walls, and breaking windows); hearing a parent threatening to hurt the other parent; physical abuse (especially when it's explained as "discipline"); and sexual violence. They can thrive in environments where they wonder if a parent will still be there when they get home from school, and in homes where they get a couple of hours of sleep at night because they awaken and are ready to jump in and protect a parent. Their natural abilities allow them to survive all that stuff with no negative consequences.

So it makes sense to stay in your marriage and provide them with a home and two parents.

It actually helps your marriage to keep the children around. You see, as children they will believe that their parents' marital problems are their fault. Therefore, your children will do their best to help you parents fix your relationship. You can reinforce that natural instinct by blaming them for your problems.

So by all means, stay together because it helps your kids.

ON SECOND THOUGHT . . .

This is not a black-and-white situation. A careful assessment is required, rather than a belief that staying in a marriage is always the best option. You may not be doing them any favors by staying in your marriage.

Safety and nurturance are not niceties that some children get to enjoy; they are crucial for healthy human development. For many reasons not all children have the same level of resilience; they don't all have the same ability to push back or recover from the stress of living with dysfunctional parents. Depending on their physical traits and their level of maturity they may not be well-equipped to protect themselves.

Being a child already has a natural vulnerability, but living in a home where they are susceptible to regular loud arguments, violence, abuse, neglect, fear, and anxiety increases their vulnerability, their self-blame, and has long-lasting detrimental consequences.

Further damage is done when parents blame their children and don't take personal responsibility for their marital behavior. Even as adults those children can persist in the belief that they are the cause of other people's problems, and fall deeper into shame.

It also damages their perceptions and expectations of marriage and other healthy relationships. They don't have a good example of what a healthy relationship looks like, and therefore may accept the same behavior from a future spouse.

It is not safe to assume that keeping your family together is best for your children.

PARTING THOUGHT

"Divorce isn't such a tragedy. A tragedy is staying in a marriage, teaching your children the wrong things about love."[1]

FOR FURTHER REFLECTION

What do your children see when they watch the interactions of their parents? Do they feel safe to be with the two of you?

What do you think is the effect on your children when they see your interactions? Does it help them or hurt them?

What are things that you can do so that your children feel safe, even if their parents are experiencing conflict? What could be the effects if your children know too much about your difficulties?

1. Weiner, *Fly Away Home*, 362.

37

There Are Several Simple Ways
to Save a Marriage

MYTHICAL THINKING

Just to be ready, let's make a list of things that you can do if your marriage is sliding downhill:

1. Start a new job. This is good because it allows you to focus your attention elsewhere. This way, you don't have to think about your marriage or pay attention to your spouse. You have a built-in reason—you have to focus on your new job.

2. Get a new home, or better yet, build a new home from scratch. This is a good option because it is something you can do together. When you are having difficulty communicating, or when it's hard for the two of you to resolve a difference of opinion, this will give you many opportunities to practice arguing and negotiating about everything from neighborhood and room layout, to furnishings, paint colors, and the finish on the bathroom fixtures.

3. Move. This option works because you realize the problem is "out there" somewhere. So if you can get away from "here," the problems will be left behind.

4. Have a baby. Nothing helps calm a marriage like the joy of a bundle of new responsibilities, new expenses, loss of sleep, and another person who is demanding your attention.

5. Have an affair. One of the favorite choices for many spouses is to look elsewhere for what's missing in the marriage. When your partner finds out about the affair, the realization will dawn about how much emptiness and pain you are experiencing, and you will be taken back with open arms and a forgiving heart. Marital bliss will be restored with no questions asked.

6. Threaten a divorce. This helps your partner feel secure in the relationship and want to invest time and energy into the marriage. The idea that it could be a waste of time, and that the decision to end the marriage is not even under their control will help to keep your emotions at a low level.

7. File for divorce. This is a commendable option, because the feeling of rejection will make your spouse want to be with you even more!

ON SECOND THOUGHT . . .

Now let's review your list, and see whether these options can deliver what you hope for.

1. New job. NO.

2. New home. NO.

3. Move. NO.

4. New baby. NO.

All of these options rely on the assumption that there is something "out there," some change in the external environment, that will rescue your relationship. This includes getting a new car, getting a new wardrobe, and changing your hair color.

A marriage is two people, regardless of their places of employment, where they live, or who lives with them. There may need to be some problem-solving which involves those things, but they are not the "cure" for relationship in distress. In general, they introduce new levels of stress rather than relieve the stress.

5. Have an affair. NO.

Again, looking outside your marriage is not a cure for your relationship, and it becomes another source of pain, blame, and shame. There may be a belief that if I can get some affirmation, or happiness, or sense of intimacy or achievement elsewhere, then the marriage will be fine. Couples in extramarital affairs usually discover the same issues exist in the new relationship *because the problem comes from inside you*, and therefore *it cannot be resolved by something outside you*.

6. Threaten for divorce. NO.

7. File for divorce. NO.

Threatening or filing for divorce are not the path to saving a marriage. They are another nail in the coffin of a relationship that is dying if not already dead.

The first and perhaps the hardest step may be to start with yourself, and consider what part you play in the significant issues which are troubling your marriage. When you've been married seven times, and five of your spouses were alcoholic, their alcoholism might not be the main problem!

The second step is to get some help, because it has become apparent that the two of you cannot do it on your own, or you would have already done so.

PARTING THOUGHT

"Affairs are just as disillusioning as marriage, and much less restful."[1]

FOR FURTHER REFLECTION

When things got stressful in your relationship, did you consider any of the options on the first list? In your mind what is the appeal for those options? If you tried them, how did they help or hurt your relationship?

When things got harder in your relationship, what things did you realize that you yourself needed to change in order to improve your relationship?

When things get more challenging in your marriage, what are some people and places where you can seek support and assistance?

---

1. McLaughlin, AZ *Quotes.*

Closing

We have considered many myths that are associated with marriage. Often what characterizes these myths is their extreme thinking. Posing a situation in your head as "either-or" tends to see the situation or its resolution in extremes: "I have to quit my job today, or stay in this miserable job for the rest of my life." Thoughts and words like *always* and *never*; *every* spouse; *total* self-sacrifice, etc. are deadly. They are red flags blowing in the winds of your distress.

Here's another thought worth bearing in mind as you make your way through life: *Virtus in medio stat,* that is, virtue lies in the middle. For example, think about the virtue of generosity. At one end of the spectrum is the extreme of being miserly—nothing is shared, everything is kept to yourself. At the other end of the spectrum is the extreme of giving everything away. That seems to be really generous, but not when others have to pay your bills, you cannot support a family, and you have no home (because you gave it away). That is not virtuous either. The true virtue of generosity lies somewhere between keeping everything for yourself and giving everything away.

Another way to step back from extreme thinking is to use the word *and*. It expresses the beliefs that: (a) you can have more than one feeling at the same time or about the same person or situation, (b) your predicaments can have more than one cause, and (c) your situations can be addressed by more than one response.

You can like someone *and* be disappointed by them at the same time. You can be sad that your friend is moving *and* happy that they will have a terrific new job. You can be angry that your children have come home several hours after curfew *and* relieved that they are safe.

Living virtuously will help you find a good partner and enjoy a reasonably happy life together. Being careful with your extreme thoughts and extreme words will avoid the extreme assumptions, feelings, and behavior found in the myths of marriage.

PARTING THOUGHT

"Wasn't marriage, like life, unstimulating and unprofitable and somewhat empty when too well ordered and protected and guarded. Wasn't it finer, more splendid, more nourishing, when it was, like life itself, a mixture of the sordid and the magnificent; of mud and stars; of earth and flowers; of love and hate and laughter and tears and ugliness and beauty and hurt."[1]

1. Ferber, *Novels of American Life.*

Bibliography

Arterburn, Steve. *AZ Quotes*. https://www.azquotes.com/quote/1521576.

Bombeck, Erma. *AZ Quotes*. https://www.azquotes.com/quote/31204.

Bovee, Christian Nestell. *AZ Quotes*. https://www.azquotes.com/quote/568080.

Brown, Brené. *AZ Quotes*. https://www.azquotes.com/quote/505551.

Chapman, Gary. *AZ Quotes*. https://www.azquotes.com/quote/1312886.

Cicero, Marcus Tullius. *AZ Quotes*. https://www.azquotes.com/quote/56685.

Deighton, Len. *London Match*. London: Hutchison, 1985.

Diller, Phyllis. *AZ Quotes*. https://www.azquotes.com/quote/946486.

Dungy, Tony. *Uncommon: Finding Your Path to Significance*. Carol Stream, IL: Tyndale House, 2011.

Ferber, Edna. *Show Boat; So Big; Cimarron: Three Living Novels of American Life*. New York: Doubleday, 1958.

Fisher, Helen. *The First Sex*, New York: Random House, 1999. https://helenfisher.com/books.html.

Framo, James L. *Explorations in Marital and Family Therapy*. New York: Springer, 1982.

Gardner, Alice. *AZ Quotes*. https://www.azquotes.com/quote/1131764.

Ghandi, Mahatma. "Interview to the Press." In *Collected Works of Mahatma Gandhi Online*, Vol. 51.

Gibran, Khalil. "On Marriage." In *The Prophet*. New York: Alfred A. Knopf, 1972.

Gottman, John M. *The Seven Principles for Making Marriage Work*. New York: Three Rivers Press, 2000.

Harris, Sydney J. *AZ Quotes*. https://www.azquotes.com/quote/125198.

Bibliography

Hendrix, Harville. *Getting the Love You Want, 20th Anniversary Edition*. New York: Macmillan, 2007.

Herbert, A. P. *AZ Quotes*. https://www.azquotes.com/quote/130486.

Landers, Ann. *The Ann Landers Encyclopedia, A to Z*. New York: Doubleday, 1978.

Landers, Ann. *AZ Quotes*. https://www.azquotes.com/quote/167596.

Larson, Doug. *AZ Quotes*. https://www.azquotes.com/quote/520646.

McIntyre, Peter. *AZ Quotes*. https://www.azquotes.com/quote/533531.

McLaughlin, Mignon. *AZ Quotes*. https://www.azquotes.com/quote/944289.

Murray, Joe. *AZ Quotes*. https://www.azquotes.com/quote/209844.

Nash, Ogden. "A Word to Husbands." In *The Best of Ogden Nash*, edited by Linell Nash Smith. Chicago: Ivan D. Ree, 2017.

Needham, Richard J. *AZ Quotes*. https://www.azquotes.com/quote/568024.

Phelps, William Lyon. *AZ Quotes*. https://www.azquotes.com/quote/946507.

Qadhi, Abu Ammaar Yasir. *AZ Quotes*. https://www.azquotes.com/quote/670484.

Ramsey Solutions. "Money, Marriage, and Communication." www.daveramsey.com/research/money-marriage-communication.

Ramsey, Dave. *The Total Money Makeover*. Nashville: Thomas Nelson, 2013.

Roberts, Cokie. *AZ Quotes*. https://www.azquotes.com/quote/527315.

Rowland, Helen. *We Should All Be So Feminine: We Should All Be Feminists*. Women Journal, 2017.

Rudner, Rita. *AZ Quotes*. https://www.azquotes.com/quote/253775.

Sawyer, Diane. *AZ Quotes*. https://www.azquotes.com/quote/520643.

Shaw, George Bernard. "Preface," *Getting Married*. 1911; Project Gutenberg, 2013. https://www.gutenberg.org/files/5604/5604-h/5604-h.htm.

Signoret, Simone. "Simone Signoret Talking to David Lewin," *Daily Mail*, 1978.

Teilhard de Chardin, Pierre. "The Evolution of Chastity." In *Toward the Future*. Translated by René Hague. New York: Harcourt Brace Jovanovich, 1973.

Tolstoy, Leo. *AZ Quotes*. https://www.azquotes.com/quote/786594.

Twain, Mark. *Mark Twain at Your Fingertips: A Book of Quotations*. North Chelmsford, MA: Courier Corporation, 2012.

von Goethe, Johann Wolfgang. *AZ Quotes*. https://www.azquotes.com/quote/378852.

Weiner Davis, Michele. *The Divorce Remedy*. New York: Simon and Schuster, 2002.

Weiner, Jennifer. *Fly Away Home*. New York: Simon and Schuster, 2010.

Wheeler, Mortimer. Quoted without attribution by Peter Hopkirk, in *Foreign Devils on the Silk Road*. London: John Murray, 1980.

Wolf, Christa. *Patterns of Childhood*, New York: Farrar, Strauss, and Giroux, 1984.

9 781666 748901